HOMING INSTINCTS

Homing Instincts

(

Dionisia **Morales**

Oregon State University Press
Corvallis

Library of Congress Cataloging-in-Publication Data

Names: Morales, Dionisia, author.
Title: Homing instincts / Dionisia Morales.
Description: Corvallis : Oregon State University Press, 2018.
Identifiers: LCCN 2018002728 | ISBN 9780870719189 (paperback)
Subjects: LCSH: Morales, Dionisia. | Morales, Dionisia—Homes and
    haunts. | Women authors, American—Biography. | Home. | Migra-
    tion, Internal—United States. | Place attachment. | Identity (Psychol-
    ogy) | BISAC: LITERARY COLLECTIONS / Essays. | BIOGRA-
    PHY & AUTOBIOGRAPHY / Personal Memoirs.
Classification: LCC PS3613.O6655 A6 2018 | DDC 814/.6—dc23
LC record available at https://lccn.loc.gov/2018002728

♾This paper meets the requirements of ANSI/NISO Z39.48-1992
(Permanence of Paper).

Oregon State University Press
121 The Valley Library
Corvallis OR 97331-4501
541-737-3166 • fax 541-737-3170
www.osupress.oregonstate.edu

☾ Contents

⟪ Acknowledgments

Essays from this collection have appeared previously in the following publications: "You Are Here" in *The MacGuffin*; "The Newcomers" in *Oregon Humanities Magazine*; "The Waffle Iron" [formerly "The Gift"] in *Pembroke Magazine*; "First Kitchen" in *Blue Earth Review*; "Catch Me, I'm Falling" and "Homing Instincts" in *Hunger Mountain*; "Blue Means Water" section 2 in *South Dakota Review* and section 3 [formerly "Continental Divide"] in *Crab Orchard Review*; "Conversations About Bees" in *Camas Magazine*; "Home at the Heart" in *Colorado Review*; and "A Lingering Sense of Place" in *Blue Mesa Review*.

At the Hotel Maestral, Zlatko leaned forward in his chair, took a sip of wine, and described in broken German the idiosyncrasies of his family's history: his grandmother was Austrian, his mother was Italian, his children are Croatian. "And me?" he said, as if delivering the punch line to a joke, "I used to be Yugoslavian." The crux of the matter was that Zlatko's family has lived in the same town for four generations; they have stayed in one place, but their nation's statehood has shifted. As we sat drinking around a small table in front of the stage in the hotel lounge, I thought about the work of cartographers, relabeling the maps of the area to redefine the meaning of "here." Unlike Zlatko, my husband, Stefan, and I led the lives of wanderers, moving from one coast of the United States to the other, uprooting our lives to cross the Atlantic each summer, only to turn back around. We'd come that night to see Zlatko perform, and he'd joined us for a drink while waiting for the two other members of his soft rock trio to unpack their instruments for the evening's first set. Zlatko lifted his glass in a solo toast. "But no matter what, Istria is our home." He laughed with a tone of resignation that is inherited, not learned. I raised my glass and laughed along with him, but with little real understanding of the complex cultural layering of this place—a triangle of land that has changed sovereignty four times in the last seventy-five years.

Sandwiched between the Gulf of Trieste to the west and the Kvarner Bay to the east, Istria is the largest peninsula in the Adriatic Sea. Shared by three countries, the bulk of the peninsula is in Croatia, a slice is in Slovenia, and a small corner belongs to Italy. Talking to Zlatko, we got our first history lesson before realizing how much there was to learn. For centuries, Istria has been conquered and partitioned, claimed and contested. Looking around the smoky lounge, I tried to pick out the locals (the people like Zlatko, who didn't need cartographers to tell them where they were from) and the tourists (the people like me, who depended on maps to find this place). But there was nothing distinctive in the way anyone leaned or laughed, nursed their drinks or tapped their feet in anticipation of the music, nothing to give away their opinions on Istria's transitions. At least I didn't think there was any sign. But what did I know? Like so many before me, I was just passing through.

Stefan and I had driven to Istria from Germany to rock climb on the region's limestone cliffs. We rendezvoused with two friends—Zlatko's brother-in-law and sister-in-law—and made Novigrad our home base. Zlatko and his wife, Jutta, had a vacation rental there, and the simple apartment was luxurious compared to our typical climbing trip accommodations, which usually involved sleeping in tents and crafting meals on a single-burner white gas camping stove. But more than just the pleasure of having four walls and indoor plumbing, the apartment also gave us a chance to spend time with Zlatko and Jutta, who showed us around Novigrad and gave us a taste of what it means to be Istrian. And that's how we found ourselves at the Hotel Maestral on a Friday night, when the preseason tourist crowd was just waking up to the possibilities of the place.

It was a ten-hour drive from where we were staying in southwestern Germany to Istria, a journey that took us east through Munich and then south through Austria and Slovenia to the Croatian border. Austria was a familiar sight; we had skied and hiked there many times. But as we passed the Austro-Slovenian border, I focused on the landscape with a sharper curiosity and noticed how the wood-clad structures in the foothills of the Alps gradually ceded to stone constructions. I wondered: In the hundred kilometers from Spittal an der Drau to Kranj, what was so different about people's lives—their routines and necessities—that led them to build such different dwellings? Looking at the map, I traced my finger along our route and felt the uncertainty that comes from not being able to pronounce the names of the places you are passing: Hrušica, Vrhnika, Hrpelje. That unfamiliarity would have been more acute and unsettling had we been traveling at anything less than highway speed; it is easy to dismiss what you don't know when it quickly disappears in your rearview mirror. In Slovenia, we headed for the western shoulder of the Istrian peninsula, barely skirting the Italian border near Trieste. When we finally crossed into Croatia and exited the highway, we slowed our pace and followed narrow winding roads that snaked through small towns, edging around centuries-old limestone buildings—some ruler-straight and others askew. The hot gleam of the grey-white walls contrasted with the deep shadows of the windows and doorways. It gave the houses an appearance that was equal parts welcoming and ominous, depending on the angle from which you approached them.

This was my first time visiting the former Yugoslavia, and initially I was skeptical about the trip. That's how I get when I can't easily build a picture of myself in a particular place. While packing, I took stock of what I knew about Croatia and quickly discovered that my knowledge was limited to a patchwork of images broadcast on network television in the 1990s. Back then, when the country fought a bloody battle for its independence, I was myopically focused on getting into graduate school and paying my rent. I remembered hearing about ethnic conflicts, war crime trials, and unexploded land mines, but I couldn't connect any of those specifics to the list of climbing areas Stefan had meticulously researched. My thoughts were crowded with impressions of war and recovery as I pushed my climbing shoes and harness into our gear bag and hesitated, wondering: Was this really where I wanted to spend my vacation? But when we crossed the border from Slovenia, I saw no signs of contentious politics, no evidence of battle for territory and ideas—not on the surface, at least. In the distance, Croatia's chalky-white karst mountains yielded to rugged valleys and picturesque rolling hills. Somewhere out there, beyond what I could detect with my naked eye, grew fields of lavender, wheat, rosemary, and rows of trees blossoming with olives and peaches. I knew they were out there because I'd read about them in our guidebook, and I believed what I'd read the way you believe any good story that is so flush with details that it builds a truth. Any lingering fears of land mines or thoughts of ethnic strife were calmed by those images and then washed away by the sight of the blue-green Adriatic Sea. I stared out across the water, and the liquid landscape invited my mind to arrive.

Sitting with Zlatko in the smoky hotel lounge, I noticed how he rested a protective arm around the hard case of his Fender electric guitar. Jutta had told us in the car that it is a special occasion whenever Zlatko brings out the Fender, which is heavier than his other guitars and hangs across his body in a way that aggravates his back. I felt honored to see him perform with it. It was clearly a prized possession. American imports like this were almost impossible to come by when Yugoslavia was behind the Iron Curtain, and during the war for independence, foreign-made leisure items were still out of reach for most people because they were cost prohibitive. Things had changed dramatically since then and were about to change again: Croatia was busily preparing for its accession into the European Union. When I asked Zlatko what he thought about Croatia becoming one of the European Union member states, he shrugged his shoulders and said, "What is there to think about?" Then he drained his glass and gestured to his bandmates that it was time to start the show.

On stage, Zlatko introduced the members of his group. Hearing his voice over the speakers, the hotel guests filtered out of the dining room and took seats at tables around the stage or milled near the bar. There was a feeling of excitement in the room as Zlatko strapped on his guitar and struck the opening chords. Couples took to the dance floor and swung each other with an untapped and urgent energy, as though everything might change in an instant. The band played a medley of Adriano Celentano hits, and Zlatko crooned "Non Esiste L'Amor" and "Pregheró" in Italian. He had learned Croatian in school, but not until he was nine years old; Italian was the language he'd grown up speaking at home. The original lyrics for "Volare" rolled off his tongue, giving me new appreciation for a song that I only ever had associated with kitschy Chrysler commercials from the 1970s. Between songs, Zlatko leaned into the microphone and joked with the regulars, gesturing that everyone should take a turn on the dance floor. He spoke mostly in Istrian dialect, an Italo-Croatian combination of vocabulary and tonalities, but dipped fluidly into proper Italian and Croatian, depending on what he was saying and whom he was addressing. For our benefit, he translated a few side comments into German but wasn't convincing enough to get us to dance. I wondered: Had he learned German to converse with his grandparents or to better map the heart of the woman he loved? Born and raised in Germany, Jutta was his Black Forest bride. Zlatko's mixing and matching of languages made space for everyone in the room to understand and be heard. Working the room like this came naturally to him, as though it was the way things had always been done.

《

The Illyrian tribes of the Histri originally settled Istria during the Bronze Age, around 1500 years before the age of Christ. You can still find remnants of their culture today, the most famous of which are the hill-forts, which were built with large stone blocks using a mortarless technique. Farmers still raise Boskarin, the grey and white longhorn cattle that once plowed fields and towed stones, and several dialects endure to bind the people with the words and stories of their ancestors. The Romans conquered Istria around 177 BCE and occupied the peninsula until the fall of the Roman Empire in 476 CE. In the centuries that followed, Istria's sovereign rule changed hands through war and invasion. The fertile soil and protected harbors were magnets for the Frankish, Venetian, French, Austrian, Italian, and Yugoslavian empires. Foreign merchants and armies were eager to control this geographic jewel that, because of its position at the crossroads of major land and sea trade routes of Central Europe, provided both economic and military advantage. If strategic location was a primary motivation for occupying Istria, tourism was its desirable by-product. The white sand beaches and glistening, aquamarine vistas were choice locales for some of history's wealthiest travelers. Tourism in Istria dates at least as far back as the Roman Empire, when Rome's influential citizens were drawn to cities like Pula at Istria's southern tip, where they built luxury summer houses along the shores of the peninsula.

In Pula, the Roman emperor Vespasian ordered the expansion of the city's arena to accommodate twenty thousand spectators for gladiator fights. First built in wood and later converted to stone, it is an immensity of creamy white, rising on a hill and framed against an aqueous background. As the Romans sailed toward the Istrian coast, the arena—appearing and disappearing with the rise and fall of their boats on the sea—must have been a beacon drawing them in a steady line east. Like the remnants of roads, aqueducts, and domed basilicas across central Europe and the near East, the arena is a symbol of Rome's might and ingenuity. But in Pula, it also represents the love of an emperor and a maiden. According to legend, Antonia Cenida, a daughter of Istria, stole Vespasian's heart, and it was she who convinced him to expand the monument as a lasting symbol of their devotion to one another. It is said that Cenida enticed Vespasian with the essence of lavender and used its intoxicating scent to persuade him to dedicate the arena to their love. Whether Vespasian's vision was to a provide a better place of leisure for Roman soldiers or create a token of his affection, the structure's soaring pillars remain as much a part of the landscape as the nested petals of lavender flowers that spring to life along windy roadsides and in the gardens of stone houses.

Few tourists can resist the draw of the arena when visiting Pula. When we stopped there, I ran a hand along one of the exterior columns. Centuries of visitors have tamed the rough edges of the steps to a glassy sheen because limestone turns to marble with heat and pressure. From a distance, the columns appear glossy, but up close they are pitted; still pressed into service, the stone has lost none of its elemental texture. Reaching my arms around one of the columns, I thought about how they defy easy definitions of "now" and "then" and "us" and "them." The Romans were only one society of many that claimed Istria and then left, and the Istrians did more than just weather the influx of conquerors, settlers, and treasure seekers. With each successive wave of new arrivals, the Istrians claimed the best parts of what other cultures left behind—the structures and stories, the dialects and delicacies. Conflict and social instability nearly erased the native Histri, but they learned to adapt and change, and that mutability became a part of who they are.

were out of view, we heard the echoes of their conversations reverberating off the stone walls. The sounds, disembodied and rebounding around us, made me feel like we were climbing in a place possessed by ghosts. When I shared this idea with Stefan, he reassured me that I was only hearing the voices of other climbers and pointed out that they could hear us too. "I know," I said, making the first moves on the route, focusing now on the sequence of holds on the pitted face of the rock.

Every climber has a favorite kind of rock. Some like the bite of granite or the pebbly crimps of tuff. Fans of basalt are drawn to its razor-thin edges and crack systems. I like limestone when the pockets still have sharp edges and texture, but I shy away from routes that have become slick after so many climbers have polished the stone with the touch and heat of their feet and hands. As rock formations go, limestone is only a thin crust over the surface of the Earth. Seeing walls of it rise out of the Vinkuran quarry floor in massive, monolithic outcroppings makes it easy to forget that limestone is not among the more durable types of bedrock. Unlike the igneous and metamorphic rocks that are forged from extreme volcanic and tectonic forces, limestone is made through sedimentation of fragments of stone, coral, and the skeletal remains of sea organisms that have been compacted by pressure and then carved and carried away by glaciers, wind, and waves.

Climbing that day, we pulled on and moved past fossils embedded in the routes. Toward evening, as we prepared to hike out, I picked up a rock fragment, about the size and shape of my fingernail, with a shellfish fossil at its center. A small mollusk had been carried off and entombed in layers of mineral-rich mud before being deposited here. I followed the spiral wind of its shape to a pinpoint at its center. Calcium carbonate had been leached from the mollusk's shell, preserving the outline of its appearance and elevating a humble invertebrate to an imprint of time and travel. Even though we'd seen these everywhere all day, I felt guilty taking it, as though I were disturbing a natural order. "Look," I said, showing the shard to Stefan, hoping for a sign from him about the ethics of palming the stone. He admired its intricacy and delicacy, but didn't say much more. I slipped the stone into my pocket and justified my thievery by telling myself I was only carrying this vestige of the past a little further than it had already come. Like so many other things in Istria, it likely was not originally from here, anyway.

At the end of the day, arms and legs spent from climbing, we packed our gear into the car and headed back to Novigrad to meet Zlatko and Jutta for dinner. That evening, as I strolled with Jutta along the harbor, she told me that the city had had many names over the centuries. When the Roman citizens of Emona fled the Huns, some of them made it to current-day Novigrad and renamed it Aemonia or "Second Emona." During the fifth and sixth centuries the city was called Neapolis and later Civitas Nova, both meaning "New City." In its rich and turbulent past, this city had been new to its many masters.

When we passed a group of men, Jutta caught a fragment of their conversation. "Local carpenters, not tourists," she said. "There is always work to do before the tourists come." I detected both relief and disappointment in her voice. We'd planned our trip for just before Easter, when temperatures were cool enough in the morning to climb in the sun and warm enough in the late afternoon to try routes in the shade. Unlike the beachgoers, who would arrive within a few weeks, we didn't plan on doing any swimming and were not bothered by the fact that it was still too cold to take a dip in the sea. We relished the uncrowded, off-peak days with a quiet greediness. We woke each morning and claimed our space, confident we'd climb, eat, and stroll undisturbed. Walking past empty alleys and cafés, Jutta and I stopped at an ice cream shop. There was no line, and the ice cream vendor waited patiently while I decided which flavors I wanted. His expression was attentive but unanimated, as though his mind were on other things. My business must have seemed inconsequential compared to the spring and summer crowds he was hoping for. As soon as I handed him my money, he disappeared mechanically behind the counter.

When I asked Jutta about life in Novigrad during the winter, she told me how, by the end of August, the locals are ready to reclaim their home. "But," she said, "by the end of January everyone is looking ahead to the next season." Her tone betrayed the benefits and liabilities of living in a coveted destination—people come, whether or not you invite them, and then it's not always easy to insist that they leave. We finished our ice cream standing in front of a row of moored fishing boats. Swabbed, empty, and idle, they bobbed gently in the water. From a distance they looked like picturesque props, adding color and distinction to the edge between land and sea. But up close I recognized them as tools, faded and marred from use, not vanity. The fishermen set out each night and sorted, packed, and sold their catch before sunup. A heavy, blue latex glove mounted on a slim pole at the rear of one of the rigs reminded me that real work was done here. It's an ancestral task, carried out under cover of darkness, during the slumber of conquerors, occupiers, and vacationers—all of them, in their own way, just passing through. This is what remains over the course of history, the layers of paint and varnish on a hull, scraped and patched just enough to be seaworthy.

The next day we headed toward Rovinj to climb in Limski Kanal. We hiked down to the base of an escarpment with sheltering trees and a view of the estuary. "Limski," which comes from the Latin word meaning "limit," refers to the area's proximity to the border of Dalmatia and Italia, two Roman provinces. Wherever we went were reminders of the shifting lines between "yours" and "ours." That evening, before heading back to Novigrad, we stopped to buy souvenirs at a roadside stand. A woman greeted us and pointed to her specialties—dried meats, cheeses, fresh bread, and wines. Wanting to bring something special back for Stefan's family in Germany, I asked, "Are all of your things traditional for Croatia?"

"No. None," she said. "But they are all Istrian."

Her tone was gently scolding and proud, her expression patient and expectant.

"Of course," I said talking more to myself than to the woman. How could I have forgotten so quickly what Zlatko had tried to teach us that night at the hotel?

We bought a bottle of muscatel, a small wheel of raw milk sheep cheese, and a bottle of lavender-infused olive oil to give as gifts, and a loaf of bread and dried ham to eat in the car on the drive back to Novigrad. Similar to Italian prosciutto, Istrian ham is a delicacy that has the distinctive flavor of the region. Dried in the bora, a strong, cold, northeast wind, it is flavored with the salt of the Adriatic, which suffuses the meat with the most primal elements of the peninsula. As soon as we drove away from the stand, I tore into the bread and ham. Starved after a long day of climbing in the sun, I ate with ravenous hunger, barely taking time to enjoy the rich aroma and flavor of the meat. I was too focused on my growling stomach to recognize that I was consuming a part of the past, a literal and philosophical taste of Istria as it has always been, as Zlatko had tried to describe it. But maybe I am naïve in thinking that my inattention had anything to do with missing out on that kind of pleasure, which is often uniquely reserved for the people who have inherited a place and call it home.

As we neared Novigrad, I realized that ours was the lone car on a new branch of highway. The names of the towns on the highway signs were crossed out with orange and black tape, giving the drive an eerie, almost post-apocalyptic vibe, as if there were nowhere left to go and no one left to get there. Jutta and Zlatko later told us that that section of the highway wasn't officially open, but people could access the on- and off-ramps while the construction crews were finishing cosmetic details. The roadwork was one of many improvements that were part of Croatia's bid for accession into the European Union. Among the criteria to be part of the EU were financial stability, a functioning market economy, stable institutions guaranteeing the rights of law, and an established infrastructure. According to public statements made by the European Commission, membership in the European Union would position Croatia to have a stronger influence in the world and better chances for dealing with the consequences of globalization. Although I never asked him, I don't doubt that Zlatko would have shrugged his shoulders at such a proclamation and said, "And what's new about that?"

While on the deserted section of highway, we cruised through a tollbooth without paying because the barrier was up and no one was at the collection station; workmen were on the roof, installing decorative corrugated metal panels. The workmen didn't seem to notice our passing, and it felt as though the highway wasn't for us, not really, not yet. They were busy preparing for the waves of cars and trucks destined to come, transporting tourists and trade. There was no trace yet of that surge, but the workmen toiled in the setting sun as though the invasion might arrive at any moment and they wanted to be ready when it did.

ℂ The Newcomers

I set out for Oregon like many of the first immigrants to the West, lured by the prospect of a new beginning. Until that point, I had lived mostly in cities in the eastern United States and had no reason to believe that the geography of my life would be defined by anything other than high-rise buildings and the anonymous press of crowds. But a month-long wilderness experience in the Colorado Rockies when I was twenty-eight presented a new landscape of possibilities. I had arrived in stiff leather boots, making me a conspicuous novice on the trip, and the thirty days were a taxing blur of hauling, river fording, glissading, and orienteering. But each evening, stomping my feet against the cold, I witnessed the urgent illumination of alpenglow that stretched the last of the day's light in saturated pinks and yellows across the snowcapped peaks. I didn't know it then, but in those moments my internal compass started to drift west.

A year later, I took a job three thousand miles from my then home in Boston to work for the Oregon Department of Education. One day, my boss, Bill, overheard me say that I had never hunted. An Oregon-born hunter, Bill often said that people like me—softhearted East Coast émigrés—were invading the rugged spaces of the West and diluting its ways. That day, he began a speech about the union of land, life, and sacrifice in the "you have a lot to learn, city girl" tone he often used with me.

He told me he had hunted since boyhood, scrambling in the backcountry after white-tailed deer. Raised in the upper Deschutes River basin of Central Oregon, Bill's earliest memories were the taste of high desert grit and the sweet scent of sage. I never saw him in a cowboy hat, but I didn't doubt he owned a few, well worn against the swelter of his youth. I pictured him peeking out from beneath a wide brim, his eyes drawn up for a sun-spotted view of the Cascade Mountains. I doubt his gaze ever stayed long above tree line, focusing instead on the forested foothills of pine and fir, where the big game forages, ruts, and rears.

I knew that rugged country as well as a newcomer could. When I'd first arrived in Oregon, I'd taken up rock climbing, eager to find community in the outdoors. Bill dismissed the artifice of the sport, saying that nothing about basic survival ever required clinging to a rock. It seemed like a fad to him, just another passing trend, something he could wait out. But I told him that a new generation of climbers had put Oregon on the map as a preeminent sport-climbing destination. People came from all over the world to scale the state's volcanic tuff and basalt walls, and many never left, making a home in the shadows of the desert canyons. They were people like me, with unconventional preferences, who were shaping a new sense of place.

As if wanting to stem that tide, even in some small way, Bill devoted a lunch hour to teaching me about hunting. I was worried at first. I anticipated vivid descriptions of the kick of the rifle butt, the rip of the bullet through flesh, the pungent mix of gun smoke, blood, and evergreen. But he surprised me, mostly talking about the art of stepping silently through favorite hunting grounds. I learned that in Oregon it is unlawful to waste meat in the field by butchering only the choice cuts. So with an animal caught in the cross hairs, a hunter has to make a

split-second computation, calculating the likelihood of hauling a prize through the bush and back to the car. The message
transmits from the brain to the trigger finger and requires a
binary conclusion—fire or hold.

I saw a faint shadow of common ground in Bill's description
and told him how, in a similar way, climbers take aim on a route,
narrowing their focus on the features immediately within reach
and composing a sequence of moves that match terrain to stami-
na. Hesitation or miscalculation can end in falls. Most drops
come to a safe halt when the slack in the rope pulls tight against
the climber's harness, but others have tragic outcomes, leaving
climbers' bodies shattered, split, and hemorrhaging. He agreed
when I said that as different as our pastimes were, we were both
drawn to the edgy urgency of nature—for him it was carried
as the last heat of life rising as steam from a kill and for me it
resonated through taut suspension in the crisp, high desert air.

Not long ago, I heard reported on the radio that hunting
remains a strong tradition in rural western states. I don't doubt
that Bill would have used that fact as ammunition in one of
our tongue-in-cheek disputes about the merits and liabilities
of change. Thinking about that report now, I suspect that newcomers like me—leaving lives in big cities for adventures in
open spaces—won't be the ones to perpetuate hunting as a tradition. Because I do not hunt, it is less likely that my children
will hunt; and because I had my children in climbing harnesses
by the age of five, it is more likely they will be scaling Oregon
rock long after I'm gone. It is evidence that changes—signif-
icant or small—can come in waves that saturate generations.

In this sense, Bill was right to think that people like me were
diluting the "old ways." But outrage about an evolving present is dangerous; it prevents us from recognizing or remem-
bering patterns from the past. Oregon has long been a land of
newcomers, beginning with the first wagons that traversed the
Cascade Mountains and descended into the Willamette Val-

ley, loaded with supplies and the principle of manifest destiny. When the federal government relocated Central Oregon Native Americans to reservations, they apportioned the tracts of land that would eventually become the sage-strewn subdivision where Bill grew up. I think that a sense of place can become so ingrained in us that we forget that things weren't always how they now appear. It is convenient to ignore that we were all newcomers at some point, that we all share the responsibility for pressing the boundaries between "what was" and "what is."

I met Bill during my first extended stay in Oregon, one that lasted four years. After that, Stefan and I left the state to be closer to family and had our kids on the East Coast. But we quickly grew restless there and, with the children still in diapers, we returned to the West. A few weeks after we resumed our life in the Willamette Valley, Bill stopped by our house. While we sat and talked, we watched my two toddlers construct elaborate settlements out of cardboard moving boxes and pillows. Like me, they were born three thousand miles away, but unlike me, their lasting memories would be of Oregon's verdant valleys and high desert plateau. This would be the place my children would always call home; this would be the place they would navigate back to if they ever wandered and lost their bearings.

On weekends, I still climb the stone towers of Central Oregon. Suspended by rope and harness above the red smudge of the high desert floor, I can lean back to admire the chain of volcanic rock. The yellow, orange, and brown mottle has the look of baked clay and appears smooth from a distance. But up close, with hands on holds, it bites with sharp edges through skin and callus. Gazing across the plateau, I often wonder how these rock outcrops must have appeared to the pioneers from their wagons. Looking up at the terracotta walls while they grazed their animals on bunchgrass, more than one must have asked, *What strange, new place is this? And how will we survive here?*

⟪   A Homesteader's Packing List

The Waffle Iron

The first time I moved across the country, it was to live with a college boyfriend for the summer, and on one of our first San Francisco Saturdays together, I'd awoken knowing only one thing: I wanted plain, round waffles—fresh, not frozen—with syrup. I'd had this kind of singular certainty before—sometimes it was related to a dream or a joke or a conversation, but this time it presented as a craving. He indulged me with kisses and humor, and we threw on our clothes as if in a race and set off on a quest.

We went from one breakfast joint to another, scanning the menus. We found tricked-out versions of what I wanted—deep-pocketed Belgian waffles with strawberries and powdered sugar, and Scandinavian waffles with delicately linked hearts, but not the plain kind. The farther we walked, the more I wanted them. From our apartment in The Haight to Noe Valley and back, I grew more determined, and that single-mindedness was its own brand of bliss. But with each café we passed, he turned more impatient and brooding, as if he'd been set up to fail. After we'd almost come full circle, he had his great idea: "We can buy a waffle iron." The hardware store down the street from our apartment sold them. I was giddy carrying the box home, holding a promise. He, on the other hand, fretted that the morning had been a waste of time. I told him sometimes it's enough to know exactly what you want, even if you don't get it. He eyed me the way he did when he wasn't sure if he could trust me. That look always made me skittish, made me wonder whether I should apologize. "This is brilliant," I said, tapping on the box of the new waffle iron he'd just bought for me.

He wasn't my first boyfriend, but he was the first man in my life. When we met, I was a freshman in college and he was a senior; he was captain of the track team and I was nobody in particular. I felt sure he would never choose me. But a year after he graduated, a chance encounter and a tender embrace ignited a romance. I went back to school on the East Coast and he moved to the West Coast; we traded passionate, long-distance calls and letters. I marveled at his handwriting, compact and aligned, and wondered whether he condensed his printing to concentrate his ideas or hide his meaning. I told him tales of angels and demons, and he struggled to sort my truth from my fiction. Because I thought ours was a kind of Cinderella story, I was surprised when another man stole my heart. Fairy tales only have one Prince Charming for a reason—a second suitor confounds the happy ending. I didn't leave my boyfriend for the other man, but confessed my confusion about whom I really wanted. Looking back, I understand how such an uncertainty—however fleeting—irrevocably wounds and gives mundane tasks, like breakfast, a sense of consequence and weight. "I should have thought of buying the waffle iron earlier," he said, self-scolding as he closed the door to the apartment.

I took the box straight to the kitchen and unpacked it. That's when we realized that we were out of flour and eggs. We were too tired and hungry to go back out and buy waffle ingredients, so we ate whatever was lying around. His shoulders slouched as we rummaged for bread and cheese. He said he was sorry, even though no one was to blame. I told him there was no reason to apologize, that satisfaction can come from refusing to compromise. I didn't think he believed me so I put my arms around him and pressed my head to his chest. "Thank you for the waffle iron," I said, with only the faintest notion of how the whole morning had been a gift.

Long after I'd left San Francisco and he'd left me, I carried that waffle iron, grease-covered from use, from one city to the next, and in and out of relationships. It was a steady reminder of how I'd once squinted into the California sun, sated with an incontrovertible vision of desire.

The TV

A few years after my stay in California, I broke the news to my family that I planned to move to Portland, Oregon. We were gathered for Christmas at my parent's apartment in New York City. I told them I didn't want to marry the man I was living with in Boston (even though everyone thought that was the next, best step) and I didn't want to lose the gritty taste of confidence I'd gained after spending thirty days on a guided wilderness trip (which I'd taken to put distance between me and the man I didn't want to marry). After I'd returned from the wilderness, I hadn't washed the jacket I'd worn day and night for a month because the pungent scent of pressed sweat, cooking oil, and iodine reminded me that everything that mattered didn't always happen in a city. I pulled out my reasons for moving like cards up my sleeve, but there was no trick to distract from the fact that I knew no one where I was headed—not in Portland or in Oregon or in the Pacific Northwest. When my explanations for moving failed to convince, I resorted to platitudes ("change is good" and "adventure builds character") that stuck to the roof of my mouth like taffy, sugary and chewy with false purpose. Nothing I said swayed my mother. She thought I was running away from an old life; I thought I was running toward a new one.

The country never felt so wide as when my plane was wheels-up and clearing the runway at John F. Kennedy International Airport. I traced a line from right to left on my mental map of the continent and thought about the promises I'd made to my mother: I wouldn't mistake unhappiness for necessity. I wouldn't hesitate to call at any hour. I wouldn't be too proud to come back. But I knew I couldn't keep those promises if I had any hope of falling in love with new people and new places, because those promises would make it too easy to go home. A few months before my move, I'd traveled to Portland for a quick trip to start looking for a job. I met and talked to as many people as I could and gathered from my conversations that Portlanders spent their free time playing in the mountains, rivers, forests, and high desert. It made me want to learn to rock climb and snowboard and convinced me that if I wanted to reinvent my life, I couldn't hide in my apartment retreating vicariously into the lives of sitcom characters. My logic was this: if I couldn't spend nights eating alone in front of a screen, it would be easier to force myself to "get out there" and "make a go of it." So, with New York City vanishing in the tail wind, I made a promise to myself that was different from the ones I'd made to my mother. It was one that I considered more relevant to the fresh start I was looking for: I wouldn't buy a TV.

Instead, within a few weeks of arriving, I bought a mountain bike, a sleeping bag, a tent, a climbing harness, and a camping stove—all things I'd never owned before. I got a membership at the local climbing gym. I went on Friday night group bike rides. With the entrance to Forest Park only a few blocks from my apartment, I took solo walks in the shadowy understory of towering evergreens and tried to convince myself I wasn't afraid of being alone in the woods. It took practice to calm my New York City instincts, which translated isolation into danger. I picked up jargon, learning words like "endo" (going over your handle bars) and "agro" (describing a climb that is intense). I tried to feel comfortable with this new language, but the words often stalled behind my teeth, not yet mine to own and utter. When I called my mother, I talked mostly about my job, an easy recitation of projects and deadlines. But when she asked whether I was making friends, I struggled to explain how being a beginner at everything made me like an uninvited guest at a party who'd shown up without a gift. The people I biked and climbed with were generous, sharing their time and know-how, but I didn't get invitations to join them on weekends when they wanted to ride or climb something difficult. I typically spent Saturdays and Sundays by myself cleaning, cooking, or walking around my neighborhood. Then, after months of Friday nights with nothing planned, I broke my promise and, at ten-thirty at night, went shopping for a TV. I got to the store just before it closed.

Fred Meyer was one of my favorite parts of Portland because there was no place like it in New York City, no place where you could buy cake mix, eggs, hex wrenches, toothpaste, shoe polish, and a pressure cooker before picking up a birthday card and your prescription on the way out. The salesman in the electronics department looked weary when he saw me slouching toward the wall of TVs. He didn't offer any help; I didn't ask. Instead, I bent down to read the tags on the display models. I considered my options: Zenith, Sony, Samsung, or Panasonic. I debated the features: integrated VCR, concealed controls, automatic channel scan, or wood-grain cabinet. I don't know why I bothered with the tags; I only really cared about one thing. I held my arms around each TV in my price range and picked the one I thought I could carry. This was essential because as a stereotypical native New Yorker, I didn't have a car or know how to drive. And as a newcomer to Portland, I didn't have any friends I could call to help me.

"The store closes in a few minutes," the salesman said.

I pointed to a Sony set. "I'll take this one."

He looked at me and tipped his head from side to side, like a kid trying to see if I was hiding a surprise behind my back. I let my hands fall to my waist.

"I'll get a cart," he said, and disappeared behind a display.

He returned pushing a shopping cart with a box that was much bigger than the TV I'd measured with my body. When I'd chosen the model, I hadn't accounted for the added girth of the packaging. I didn't have to put my arms around the box to know that I couldn't carry it on my own. I ran my eyes over it, trying to see whether it had cutout handles. It didn't. The salesman nudged the cart in my direction, but I didn't take it right away. An announcement came over the address system. "Attention shoppers ..." It was five minutes to eleven. I thanked him for his help and started pushing the cart down the aisle toward the registers. Cardboard corners jutted over the sides of the cart. I balanced a hand on top of the box not because it felt like it might tip over but because it gave the illusion that I was in control. Images flashed through my mind of other poorly proportioned loads—mothers pushing school-age children in sagging umbrella strollers, cartoon characters transporting baby elephants in wheelbarrows, movers hauling pianos on hand trucks—when really what I should have been focused on was the question I'd tried to measure with my arms: How was I going to get this TV home?

A young man with glasses stood by the only open checkout. I was one of the last customers in the store. He waved me over.

After scanning the price off the box he said, "If you pull your car around, I'll load it up."

"No thanks," I said while running my debit card, "I don't have a car."

The cashier finished ringing up the sale and waited for the receipt to print. And then, as though he thought he'd misheard me, he said, "Oh?"

His monosyllable didn't have the knockout precision of, say, "How the hell do you expect to get this thing home?" or "What's your problem?" but it was enough to make me study the speckled pattern on the floor and wonder whether his tone was polite or mocking. As I reached out to take the receipt from him, I wished he'd been more obviously judgmental. Then I could have said, "I don't have to put up with this," and after standing my ground until a manager gave me a refund, I could have used my protest as a diversion to flee the store without the box I couldn't carry, and I could have forgotten how, just a few minutes before, it had seemed like a good idea to buy a TV in the middle of the night at a supermarket. That scenario seemed more desirable than the one I was actually faced with: I not only had purchased a TV that I couldn't transport but also had broken the one promise I'd made to myself. The cashier smiled and said, "Have a good night." I folded the slip of paper into my coat pocket, put both hands on the handle of the shopping cart, and thought, "Now what?"

As I made my way to the exit, I didn't think about the smooth sides of the box that were impossible to grip. I didn't think about how, at the age of sixteen, getting my driver's license had been the furthest thing from my mind and that even now, thirteen years later, I still didn't see the need to drive or own a car, except of course, in moments like this, when you have a big box to haul. I didn't think about the sign prohibiting shoppers from taking carts beyond the parking lot or that that was my only option. I didn't think about how I'd need to maneuver the cart up and down the curbs for three blocks, get it around the sharp corner in the alley entrance to my building, fit it into the elevator and through my front door, and then edge the box from the cart to my dining room table. And I didn't think about how before plugging in the TV, I would need a strict viewing schedule to prevent myself from becoming a hermit, hypnotized by other people's lives going by on a small screen.

What I did think about was the moment from the year before, when I was still deciding whether I should move, and a friend gave me this advice on figuring out whether or not I could be happy living in Portland. He'd said: visit in winter when it's raining, wake up early, skip breakfast, forgo coffee, walk around downtown on an empty stomach without an umbrella until lunchtime, go to the 24-Hour Church of Elvis, head over to NikeTown and wander around the store for an hour. "That's your survival test," he'd said. "If you do that and still like the city, it will work." On my week-long job-hunting trip before moving, I followed his instructions because I didn't have any better way to figure out where I belonged. When I'd completed the test, I stood wet, hungry, and giddy in the Nike flagship store. "Why not live here?" I thought and returned to the East Coast just long enough to give notice at my job and pack. A few months later, I arrived back in Portland, this time on a one-way ticket.

The automatic doors to Fred Meyer were set to let the last customers out and no one else in. I pushed the shopping cart into the night and closed the distance to the perimeter of the parking lot. I didn't look back, only ahead, and rolled past the signs warning about taking shopping carts off the premises. I edged toward home, each step broadcasting a metallic rattle, and pushed as fast as I could. The cart caught and jangled on the uneven sidewalk, and when it seemed like the TV might topple, I braced a hand firmly on top of the box and leaned into the wobbly belief that I'd already proven I belonged here.

The Bed

I asked the mattress salesman if I could call my mother, and he nudged his phone in my direction.

"It's long distance," I said. He told me to dial nine.

When I picked up the receiver, he pushed his chair away from his desk a few inches and turned his head, as if to give me more privacy. I wondered whether he would have made this same gesture if I had told him that I wanted to call my boyfriend or my decorator, which, I thought, would have made me seem less lonely. But it was too late to cover any embarrassment; there was no use trying to elude these truths: I was twenty-nine years old, about to make the biggest furniture purchase yet of my life, and wanted my mother's advice. I dialed.

On a small sheet of scratch paper, written in the salesman's handwriting, was my script for the phone call: Sealy Posturepedic, full size, wrapped coils, extra firm. The phone rang three thousand miles away in my mother's New York City kitchen. I could picture her checking the simmering pots and wiping her hands on her apron before she reached for the receiver. I imagined her hoping I was on the line because every time I'd called in the last few weeks, she'd said, "I was hoping it was you." The sound of the ring tone bouncing off the high-gloss walls of her narrow, galley kitchen was more familiar to me than the hollow echo the phone made in my empty apartment.

"It's ringing," I said, out loud. Part of me wanted to hang up, the part that said, "You're too old for this."

I wasn't new to relocation; I had moved several times in the last few years, and in many ways this time was like the rest. After signing my lease, I'd called the phone and power companies, set up a bank account, mailed in change of address postcards, and scouted supermarkets. I found the cheapest place to buy heavy, plastic hangers and bought a bus map. I read the local paper, went to the Saturday farmers' market, and collected take-out menus from the little restaurants in my neighborhood. I picked up some heavy milk crates from Goodwill and used them for a makeshift bookcase, bought two small lamps, and slept on the carpet in my bedroom on a ThermaRest. When I'd lived in San Francisco, Berlin, and Boston, I'd moved to be near friends, who then introduced me around and fast-tracked invitations to parties, dinners, and concerts. This time, absent a ready-made community, I'd taken matters into my own hands. I'd made an effort to get to know my coworkers but was too shy to suggest getting together after work. They were cordial on the job but didn't invite me for drinks or a movie. So I'd joined a mountain biking group and the climbing gym, but wherever I turned everyone seemed to already know each other. I called my brother one night to complain about my boredom and loneliness. He told me to give my Oregon experiment a year.

It's hard to say what the bigger motivator was for buying the mattress and box spring—my eagerness to stop sleeping on the floor or my sense that unless I was encumbered with furniture, I wouldn't last a year, that I would set my alarm one morning and head straight for the airport and fly away, without a thought for the fruit left to rot on my kitchen counter. I'd considered buying a futon matress, but that seemd like a glorified camping pad.

"It's a big commitment," I said to my mother, when I got her on the phone.

"It's just a bed," she said.

She was right, of course, but unlike the other beds I'd ever owned, this one couldn't be rolled up and shoved into a friend's sedan. This was the kind of bed that had to be delivered.

"I guess," I said.

Each time I'd moved, my belongings had compressed into two duffel bags, a half-dozen book boxes, and the back seat of someone's car. I didn't know how I would even get rid of a box spring and mattress in a hurry. Does it come out of your security deposit if you don't dispose of it before you turn your keys in to the landlord? Folded into the side pocket of my backpack, I still had my packing list from when I left the East Coast. Besides the usual comfort clothes, I had made sure not to leave behind my blue and tan silk shirts, pleated grey skirt, blue and black blazers, fleece vest, fleece jacket with the burn hole, hiking boots, dress boots, sneakers, journals, photo albums, favorite CDs, camera, wide-angle lens, and a small jewelry box. I only had two suitcases worth of space and had selected items carefully. Whatever didn't fit was sold, tossed out, or stored in one of the closets in my parents' apartment.

I listened to my mother tell me why pillow tops weren't worth the extra money and looked across the display floor. It wasn't that I had forgotten how big mattresses and box springs were, but they took on fairy-tale proportions laid bare in the store's track lighting.

"Just buy it," my mother said. "It's time to stop sleeping on the floor."

We'd had other conversations in which she'd used different words but the same tone of voice: "It's time you settled down," or "It's time you decided what you want to do with your life," or "It's time you got married." With the long-distance line crackling between us, her impatience now took the shape of a bed.

"I guess I could always sell it," I said.

"I guess," she said.

My dilemma was an ageless one. A pioneer only carries the essentials. When the first Oregon settlers plotted a course west, the supplies in each wagon had to weigh less than two thousand pounds. Five months of food rations for a family of four accounted for most of that weight, which only left room for minimal clothing, weapons and ammunition, and few utensils and tools. But because it is hard to measure a life in pounds and ounces, families often took too much. Stoves, dressers, mirrors, rocking chairs, toys, and sewing machines were loaded in Missouri and later abandoned when the mud was deep, the oxen were tired, the wheel rims split, and survival depended on lightening the burden. To the left and right of wagon-wheel ruts, the Oregon Trail became a showcase of people's lives, witnessed through the comforts and heirlooms abandoned in the wilderness.

I thought if I ever left Oregon, this bed wasn't going to make the cut.

"You're at the store," my mother said. "You might as well."

I hung up the phone and bought the bed, not because my mother thought it was a good idea, but because I wanted to prove I could make Oregon my home and was willing to lash myself to any anchor—real or imagined—that I could find. When I handed over my credit card, I remembered something my father used to say. "Things always work out." Of course, they may not work out for the best, he'd caution, but they do eventually work out. Before I left the mattress department, I thanked the salesman for letting me use his phone and asked him to point me toward the linen department. I wanted to be ready to dress the bed as soon as it arrived. An unmade mattress and box spring have the utility of an appliance; for the money I was spending, I needed something that said, "Welcome home. Relax and stay awhile." I needed sheet sets, a comforter, a duvet cover, pillows, and shams to stake a claim.

Two deliverymen arrived the following week with the mattress and box spring. If I'd had any friends yet, maybe we would have organized a van and gone together to pick it up. Maybe we would have made a moving party out of it and laughed at the struggle to negotiate the banisters on the stairs leading to my apartment. Instead, two men from the store buzzed my apartment. I stepped aside, let them do their job, and then pulled out two tens for a tip.

By the end of my first year in Oregon, I'd accumulated more than just the TV and the mattress and box spring. I returned to the department store for other things that would never fit into a checked bag: a dinner setting for eight, framed art, a coffee table, and a couch. With each passing month I settled in more and thought less about what I wouldn't be able to take if I moved. I don't remember when I started having potluck dinners with people from the climbing gym or gave up crossing out the days on the calendar with an "X." But at some point toward the end of that year, I stopped living with a deadline. I bought wine glasses, ones with delicate bowls and stems. It felt good to cradle them in the palm of my hand. My new friends preferred beer out of the bottles, so the wine glasses never got much use, but it was still a comfort to have them, lovely in their delicate impracticality. It made me wonder what the pioneers looked forward to buying when they dreamt of their homesteads, places that existed only in their imaginations at the end of a trail they had never before traveled. Some people can reinvent themselves without putting miles between the life they have and the one they want. But the rest of us hit the road with whatever we can carry and make it up as we go along.

☾   First Kitchen

I said, "You know, the best thing for a burn is to put a slab of tofu on it." I sat on the counter, pressing an aloe vera stem between my thumb and forefinger and watching Stefan prepare a late lunch. The jelly-filled tentacle had a satisfyingly firm resistance.

Stefan skated in his socks on the cold kitchen linoleum, reaching for utensils and stirring pots. His frame was long and lean. When I had first met him a few weeks before on a rock-climbing trip, I'd barely noticed his body or how it moved. Now, the broad, relaxed slope of his shoulders and the gentle dip in the small of his back held me. I imagined the smooth bend and flex of his muscles under his clothes.

Someone who didn't know us might have gotten the wrong impression, seeing us in that kitchen. He was wearing an old, ripped T-shirt and a pair of jeans that hung low enough on his waist to suggest that he might not have on anything underneath. I was dressed in his old climbing pants rolled up on the bottom and an oversized flannel shirt. We had wet hair and flushed checks; we were starving. But appearances can be misleading. We had just returned from a hike in a downpour. This was our first real date.

"I thought aloe was supposed to be good?" he said, looking over to me. Steam rose from a pot boiling on the stove.

"It is. But tofu is better."

Stefan carried the food into the next room and set it out on the dining table—miso soup, vegetable dumplings, boiled greens, and rice with spicy tahini dressing. I was macrobiotic at the time. I was in heaven.

"Is it okay?" he said.

I smiled, thinking maybe this guy is the one, the one who really gets me, the one who just knows. It would be months until I found out that he'd orchestrated this perfect meal only after grilling my friends about what I liked to eat. He confessed this to me one night, whispering in my ear while he held me in an embrace. I laughed and laughed, and called him a sneak, but he kept my arms pinned to him. And that's when I knew my first instinct had been right.

Just as we were sitting down to eat, one of his housemates came in from the rain. He shook my hand firmly as he introduced himself. He looked us both over and then said with a wink and a smile, "Well, what have you two been up to all day?" Stefan slapped him hard across the back and explained about the hike and the rain.

"All her stuff is in the dryer," he said. "You can sit down and eat with us, but only if you are going to be nice."

His housemate set a place for himself across from me. We all smiled through the meal.

The day I met Stefan at the climbing area, I had planned on doing easy pitches with a friend. When he happened along and joined our party, I was sour because we ended up doing hard routes instead. At the end of the day he gave me his number, but I lost it. He called me twice in the following weeks, but I erased his messages—the first time on purpose and then by accident.

Looking back, it's hard to believe that he didn't make a stronger impression on me, that I wasn't more eager to talk to him right away. When he finally reached me one evening at home, I was in the middle of cooking dinner.

"Is this a good time?" he'd said.

"Well, I'm starving and I'm making squash soup. As soon as it's done, I'm going to want to get off the phone."

He didn't miss a beat. "How long do I have?" For twenty minutes we talked squarely about our likes and dislikes; we told stories about our families and made jokes. I was surprised by how unguarded I felt, by how unguarded he sounded. When the soup was ready, he ended the conversation with an invitation to hike. After I hung up the phone, I sat at the little table in my kitchen, equally hungry and edgy with anticipation, and twirled a spoon in the orange, velvety puree, watching the steam rise from the bowl.

Now, as we finished the last of the dumplings, there was a knock at the door. A woman came in and stood hesitantly in the threshold, water dripping from her coat. She shook herself off and approached the table. I felt her measuring with her eyes the distance between my chair and Stefan's. She introduced herself and I immediately wondered whether I should consider her a rival. The conversation was about some people I didn't know and something they needed. There was quick laughter; I smiled politely. When I noticed how her glance kept flashing over me, I became pleasantly conscious of my hair, still a bit damp and curling in ringlets around my face. Then I knew. She considered me *her* rival. I liked feeling that, today at least, I had the upper hand.

After she left, we cleared the dishes. I wanted to get on the road before it got dark. I had a long drive ahead and the weather was getting worse. I stepped into the bathroom off the kitchen, plucked my things from the dryer and changed. My clothes were still warm as I stood by the door to say good-bye.

"You can stay the night, if you'd rather drive in the morning?" Stefan said.

I noticed he often asked questions instead of making statements. I wasn't sure if this was a cultural quirk carried over from his German upbringing or just his quiet way of flirting. It didn't matter; it was endearing. As I gathered up my bag, I thought about sliding my hands under his shirt to feel the smooth texture of his skin. I wondered if his belly was as tanned as his forearms. I held back, uneasy about how far and how fast such a touch would lead us.

"No," I said. "I need to get home."

I reached out to hug him. Putting an arm around his shoulder, I breathed in the faint scent of rain and sweet onions. I lingered a moment and braced against the weight of him leaning down toward me. I detected no sign of the mortgage we would eventually struggle to pay or the mountains of diapers we would one day change. There was no hint of how waking up naked and safe in each other's arms would become bittersweet with the responsibilities of children, work, and household chores. Instead, the drape of his body anchored me in the present. As I pulled away, I lightly squeezed his arm. His bicep, firm and sinewy under his skin, resisted the pressure of my fingers. Then I reached for the door.

On the drive home I gripped the steering wheel with both hands to steady the car as it plowed through black patches of high water on the highway. My heart raced each time the car hydroplaned, the tires momentarily losing contact with the road. I didn't know it then, but in a few weeks Stefan and I would skid toward our first kiss. I would forget the supple flavor of our lips' first touch, but I would always remember that kitchen, dreamy in the diffuse light of cooking steam and rain-streaked windows.

⟨⟨   Catch Me, I'm Falling

I found out I was pregnant during rock-climbing season. The weekend before the test showed positive, I was clinging to the stone faces that flank central Oregon's Crooked River. That weekend, like most weekends in the late spring and early fall, Stefan and I climbed in the high desert landscape, where outcrops of terracotta-colored tuff weather in the shadow of the Cascade Range. This is where we met and courted, where we—literally—held each other's lives in our hands at the end of a rope.

Stefan and I had married earlier that spring and had just started trying to get pregnant, so in a way the news didn't come as a surprise, but the timing did. We knew from friends and books that it could take months or, in some cases, years to conceive and were unprepared when, after only a few weeks of trying, the pregnancy test signaled we were going to be parents much sooner than we'd anticipated. Had I known that that pregnancy test would mark the end of my climbing for almost two years, I might have paid closer attention to the last routes we scaled that weekend. I might have better appreciated the way a slim lip of stone can support your weight, the way your body is made longer by turning into the wall and reaching up on the diagonal. I might have taken more time to notice the rough scrape of the rock's surface against my hands and paused longer at the top of each climb to admire the view of undulating spires. If I had known that weekend that new life was taking shape in me, I might have taken greater care in observing the minute characteristics of the climbs—the pockets, rails, and shallow dishes, the edges I gripped and pushed off of, and the ones I skipped. But I thought I would have plenty of time to relish each route because I had planned on climbing to the end of the season.

Some women climb through their third trimester; there are companies that make special harnesses, which loop over the shoulders instead of cinching around the waist, for pregnant climbers. Because climbing demands keeping your hips close into the rock face and engaging the core muscles of the belly and the back, I imagine a swelling middle and spreading pelvis requires a pregnant climber to learn to work her hands and feet in new ways to compensate for an altered center of gravity. A pregnant climber needs to avoid falls that exert sudden force on the abdomen and take extra care when belaying. Deciphering what you can and can't do on the rock is always an individual decision; it's a negotiation of strength, tenacity, and risk. This triangulation of concerns is no different for a pregnant climb-er, who must also factor in possible harm to the baby. But no special harness could have swayed me from what I felt was a primal, protective instinct: in this state, I shouldn't draw my body off the ground. As soon as I found out I was pregnant, I needed no time to calculate potential hazards or shop for a new harness. My choice was simple: I decided to alight, not ascend.

The weekend before my attention turned inflexibly to my belly, I rehearsed the moves on Vomit Launch, a beautiful climb with an unfortunate name that combines balance and finesse on the lower section and tops out with a long series of strength moves to the final anchors. Each season, in addition to climbing a variety of routes on top rope, I selected a few personally challenging ones to lead. The difference between top roping and leading is the difference between hazarding a short, harmless sink into the rope and taking a long, midair drop that can result in hitting the ground. On top rope, the climber is part of a closed system in which the rope is threaded through anchors at the top of the route and the belayer takes up the slack to keep the climber on a tight line. But it takes a lead climber to get the rope to the anchors in the first place. When leading, a climber ascends the route with the rope trailing behind her, clipping into bolts for protection along the way. If she comes off the route while on lead, she'll fall the distance to the nearest clipped bolt below and then past it that same distance. When a leader falls, she is dependent on her belayer's immediate reaction to block the rope in his belay device and halt her midair descent. It happens at the speed of instinct.

The most challenging section of Vomit Launch—its crux—was a graceful balancing act of footholds. If I peeled off the rock at the crux, I would drop until the slack in the rope pulled tight between Stefan and me, and set our harnesses biting across our middles and around our thighs. In that breathless moment tumbling through the air, I would have a split second to calculate the distance between my fear of hitting the ground and my faith that Stefan would brake the rope and catch me. Then coming to an abrupt stop, panting and blinking, I would look up to measure how far I'd traveled, pausing only for a moment to consider the spectacle of dangling midair at the end of a rope. And then I would try the moves all over again. Because I had an acute fear of long falls, I first practiced moves on top rope to get them dialed in before trying the climb on lead.

In the back of every climber's mind is the fear of a ground fall. I had seen many climbers come loose from routes and drop into the spring of the rope, but I had never seen anyone hit the deck. However, one day when Stefan and I were on a climbing trip, a Life Flight helicopter circled and landed to rescue a climber who had fallen thirty feet to the ground and lay in a broken pile. Remarkably, he regained consciousness and talked to a small group of friends as they waited for the medics to come and carry him out. But all along he was bleeding into his belly and lungs, his organs shaken and split.

"I don't understand it," one of the climber's friends told us later in the parking lot. "He was awake. He seemed fine."

But really he'd been slowly dying before everyone's eyes.

"We got him to the helicopter and it seemed like everything was going to be fine." The friend stared at the ground, as if he were looking for something he'd lost.

Although I'd decided to temporarily give up climbing and stay grounded during my pregnancy, I kept active—biking and hiking—for the first twenty weeks. But sometime at the beginning of my second trimester, in a manner both painless and surreptitious, something started to go wrong. I would have stopped biking if I'd known there was a problem. I would have stopped hiking if I'd known the baby was in danger. And I certainly wouldn't have flown alone across the country to visit my family for Thanksgiving if I'd known I was risking a miscarriage.

"They found something wrong," Stefan said over the phone from three thousand miles away, the morning after I arrived at my parents' Manhattan apartment. I took the call in the kitchen and leaned into the receiver, trying to bring his voice closer. I had had an ultrasound just a few hours before boarding my flight. Because it was part of a routine check-up and there had been no prior signs of problems, Stefan and I didn't consider that the test might suggest a reason to cancel my trip. But while I was out walking, a volley of phone calls had started—from the radiologist to the obstetrician, the obstetrician to Stefan, and then finally, from Stefan to me.

"But I feel fine," I said.

"I know," he said. "You can either stay there until the baby comes or come home."

"I mean, I really feel fine."

"I know," he said. "But it could be dangerous for you to fly back. We have to decide."

In those brittle moments of our phone call, I focused on Stefan's voice. One of the most important elements in climbing is the communication between climber and belayer. When I told my parents I'd taken up climbing, my mother's greatest worry was that the rope might snap. But rarely is equipment the cause of climbing accidents; most often it's human error, and at the root of most of those errors is miscommunication between the climber and the belayer. In climbing it is important, although not always possible, for the belayer to see and hear the climber; visual cues and verbal commands help guide a safe ascent. When a climber reaches down to pull the rope to clip a bolt or calls, "Slack," the belayer responds by letting out line. When a climber's legs start to tremor, or when she says, "Watch me," the belayer responds by bracing his body and narrowing his attention. But these are only the basics. Any two climbers who have logged long days together learn to read the subtle signs of stress and confidence without exchanging a word or glance. When I belay Stefan, I am sensitive to an almost imperceptible quiver in the rope. If I look up, I might see that his body is still, and yet there is a quaking in the line, as if his core muscles are vibrating. It is almost always a prelude to a fall. And when he sees me quietly, almost unconsciously, whispering to myself, he knows that I am starting to panic. "You've got this," he'll call up to me. "You've got this." After so many years and so many routes, we know—by the way we hesitate, shake out our arms, or charge up without resting—what is needed. This intimacy of signs and signals was on my mind as I tried to imagine being away from Stefan for the remaining twenty weeks of the pregnancy.

"I can't do this here," I said. The line went still as we listened to each other breathing. "I want to come home."

We hung up so he could arrange a flight back for me on the following day. After I set down the phone, I curled up on the living room couch, holding my belly. I had only just begun to really show. My mother brought me a cup of tea and sat beside me. She stroked my hair and reassured me that everything was going to be all right, but her words rose in a swirl like the steam coming off my cup and faded into nothing. I didn't tell her that I had decided to go home, because as far as she was concerned, I was home. Instead I told her that I thought it would be better for me to see my own doctor right away and not waste time trying to find a specialist in the city. Her first reaction was adamant: "You should be here, home with your family." But when I repeated my decision to fly back to Oregon, this time with a quaking voice, she softened her tone: "I just want you to know that we can take care of you." She kept stroking my hair but stopped lobbying her point. We sat quietly for a while, and then she helped me pack.

((

In the years after college, when I moved and settled in cities and moved again, home had always been my parents' apartment. Even when my brothers and I flexed through relationships and marriages, my parents' apartment was where holidays and birthdays were celebrated. It was where we played competitive Scrabble, watched weekend championship tennis, and sat around the kitchen table arguing. During the handful of years when my brothers and I had our own apartments in New York City and lived less than a mile apart, we rarely visited each other, instead running into one another a few times a week at my parents' place. The two years that I lived six blocks from my parents, my mother visited me exactly once to bring me bread, salt, and matches—traditional symbols of bounty, flavor, and light. She arrived at my door two months after I had unpacked my last boxes because she hadn't been able find the coarse, pink sea salt she liked. When I called to tell her to just get any salt and come over, she told me she'd think about it and that I should remind her the next time I came home. *Home* can be defined as place of residence, but its real meaning is far more personal and subjective. So in telling my mother why I was risking the flight back across the country, it didn't seem the time to explain that the apartment—the place where she and my father had raised my brothers and me, the place I had always returned to—no longer felt like home. Home was now three thousand miles away where I was building the promise of my own family and living a life very different from the one I'd grown up with.

When I announced my decision to move to Oregon, it became clear my parents either had missed or chosen to ignore the fact that, over the course of many years, I'd moved to increasingly smaller locales with stronger connections to the outdoors. It was in one such place that I met Stefan, climbing for a weekend in Oregon's sage-strewn high desert. I was a beginner when we met and spent most of my time belaying him on lead and climbing on top rope. I learned quickly that a good climbing partnership takes a dual sense of faith—faith that the climber will reach the anchors and faith that the belayer will catch any fall. It was a lesson we would learn over and over as we expanded the boundaries of our relationship and eventually married.

While I had no doubt that my parents and brothers would have done everything in their power to find the best doctors and make me comfortable through the second half of my pregnancy had I decided to stay in New York City, I worried that, away from Stefan, my state of mind might kink and unravel without warning. In the years when the apartment in New York City was the center of my universe, my parents and brothers had known me better than anyone in the world. But when I moved to Oregon, when my life began to rotate around new landscapes and new interests, I changed faster than my family was aware. My mother knew that I now liked to rock climb, but she only could imagine an abstract vision of me scaling stone towers. Stefan, on the other hand, knew, based on how often I dipped my hand in my chalk bag, if I was nervous about making the next sequence of moves on a route. He also knew by the way I would clasp and unclasp my hands when I talked to him that I had made a decision—about a project for work, a vacation plan, a new haircut—but still needed time to commit to it. He was privy to my quiet ways and quirks, which was why, with our first child on the way, I didn't want to lose precious time explaining myself. When Stefan and I climbed together, he could sense when I was about to let my body tension slacken. "You've got this," he'd shout, answering my unvoiced questions about whether I should give up and come down.

((

When I arrived back in Oregon the following day, Stefan met me at the airport, and we drove straight to the hospital. The doctor explained in detail what Stefan had only been able to outline over the phone. My cervix was too weak to sustain the pregnancy; miscarriage was inevitable without surgery to stitch the cervix closed. The doctor described how my body could not contain the downward pressure of the baby and drew diagrams to illustrate the suturing technique he planned to use. I tried to focus on the details, but little penetrated the dull hum in my head. No matter what the doctor said, all I could hear was that I had failed, that my body had failed, and that because of these failures I'd almost lost the baby. I turned to Stefan for comfort and was alarmed by how frightened he looked.

Because we had discovered the problem so late, the surgery held a higher risk of preterm delivery. And if the baby came early, it could be born with any of a number of lifelong physical or cognitive disabilities. There was a lot to consider.

"If you don't want to take the chance with the surgery, you could abort the pregnancy," the doctor said.

I must have looked dumbstruck because he quickly clarified his meaning.

"That is, because we are now aware of the problem, with another pregnancy we can deal with it earlier and better."

I tried to remain absolutely still to prevent any small movement of my face or hands from being interpreted as a response. I held onto the sides of the chair.

The doctor left Stefan and me alone to discuss our options. Stefan found my hand and took it in his. I couldn't look at him because I knew I would see in his face what he thought we should do, and I worried we weren't thinking the same thing. I finally turned to him with tears and said, "It's our baby, and we'll try."

"Yes, and we'll try."

With that simple call and response, we decided to schedule the surgery immediately. I settled into the calm of the decision, not because I was sure everything was going to be all right, but because I knew that whatever came, I wouldn't have to face it alone.

A West African proverb says, "The world is a pregnant woman." It means that the world, like a pregnancy, is full of unexpected events whose outcomes are unknown. Some babies are male, and others are female. Some are healthy, and others are sickly. Some labors are easy, others are difficult; sometimes the mother dies, sometimes the child. All the books tell you that things can go wrong in a pregnancy, but the language of caution always seems remote when you are in the bloom of expectancy. You convince yourself that those other women, the ones who have complications, are not like you. Your pregnancy is going to be textbook perfect. You're going to have the innate strength to do what women have been doing for ages. But that kind of self-confidence has its roots in fear, not arrogance, because it is too terrifying to think that we might tumble from the grace of nature.

After asking a few logistical questions, Stefan and I signed the consent forms, and I was in surgery by the afternoon. In the operating room I was on my back with my feet in stirrups. The table was set at an angle with my head down and all the pressure of the pregnancy pushing toward my diaphragm. It felt like I was suddenly carrying the baby in my throat. Stefan sat beside me dressed in a sterile gown and mask and held my hand.

"Tell me a story," I said.

He looked flatly at me.

I knew that look. It was the same look he gave me when I would ask him if we could drive back to the house because I wasn't sure if I'd shut off the oven. It was the look he gave me when he wanted to say no. I started to get a small headache from the incline of the operating table. I couldn't see much of what was going on around me but could make out what sounded like a scene of activity as the nurses and the doctor prepared for the surgery. Despite the bustle, Stefan kept his eyes fixed on me.

"Then tell me all the moves I have to make to lead Vomit Launch," I said. "Tell me over and over until the surgery is done."

I saw the small creases of his forehead lift, the way they do when he's smiling.

"Lean into the bowl, off the deck," he said slowly. "Take the side pull and scramble your feet up."

"Okay," I said, closing my eyes.

"Can you see it? The light stripe running along the good foothold?"

"I see it."

"Now reach out high and right. Don't forget to swap your feet."

I remembered this early set of moves. The bowl was slightly overhung and I always wanted to move quickly to get on to the vertical face of the climb.

"Just a bit higher and you get a good rest."

Before moving to Oregon, I never imagined I could be happy anywhere other than in the anonymity and chaotic press of a big city. But the volcanic grit and high desert sage captured my imagination the first time I ventured to the east side of the Cascade Range. With my eyes closed, the holds on Vomit Launch materialized one by one, and I rebuilt the landscape a body length at a time as I ascended the climb in my mind. I didn't look down. My breathing slowed. My grip on Stefan's hand softened.

I managed to stay focused until the sound of clinking metal broke my concentration. When I looked over my curtained knees, I saw the doctor reaching for an instrument; it pulled me loose from the image of the climb, and I landed rudely in the here and now on the operating table. Deep in the center of me needles were turning; a series of carefully placed knots and stitches were keeping the baby from falling from my grasp. I felt dizzy and sick. I was losing my hold. I wanted down off the table; I wanted to leave. The spinal block they'd given me made it impossible for me to move my lower torso and legs, but I started to shake my head from side to side, pinching my lips and crying.

"It's going to be fine," Stefan said, squeezing my shoulder to get my attention. "Don't look around. Just watch me."

When I turned to face him, I saw in his eyes a willed calm.

"Let's keep going," he said. "You're almost past the bowl and then you come to the good holds and a rest before you get into the real business."

He talked me through Vomit Launch's sequence of moves a dozen times, adding more detail about the rock and the scenery with each ascent—the coarse sand of the high desert stone rubbed into our hands and knees, the intoxicating fragrance of juniper and sage radiating from the surrounding hills, the views looking down on the lazy wind of the river.

"It's so beautiful up here," he said.

When the surgery was done, the doctor came around to the side of the table to explain how everything had gone. He gestured casually to illustrate how he had pulled and stitched. His gloves were covered in blood, beaded in patches on the latex. My first thought was that the blood was my blood, and then it flashed through my mind that it might be the baby's. I felt weak at the sight of his hands, red and working in the air. What if, after all of this, we still lost the baby? What if I carried it a few weeks longer and it was stillborn? Or what if it came so early that it was sick all its life? Or too sick to survive? A shaking fright came on. My throat pursed. Stefan, still with his hand on my shoulder, stood up to focus on what the doctor was saying. I took in the conversation in pieces. The surgery had gone well. The prognosis was good. But I couldn't distill the details and struggled to steady my thoughts. I felt myself falling, unable to find anything to hang on to in the sterile, whitewashed operating room. So I shut my eyes again and pictured the sunburnt stone in my hands, imagined the caress of hot desert wind on my skin. I envisioned the climb, starting the sequence of Vomit Launch's moves from the ground. I remembered that a good climber stands up more than pulls up, setting strong feet and pushing with the legs; a good climber keeps hips close into the wall, running fingers and palms along the rock surface in search of pockets, cracks, and edges. I was a good climber. I told myself to stay focused and took a deep balancing breath. Stay focused and don't look down.

I gently rested my hand on Stefan's hand but did not interrupt him as he continued to talk to the doctor. I needed him to find out everything he could now, while it was fresh in the doctor's mind, because we would need those details later to reassure us that the surgery had gone as well as it possible could have. I knew that the information Stefan was gathering, the questions he was asking, would be important on the nights when I woke in a cold sweat, worried that every small cramp was a sign that the baby was in distress. I tried to remain absolutely still. "You've got this," I told myself over and over, working hard to believe it. "You've got this," I thought as I imagined myself clinging to the face of the climb and tightening my grip on the stone, solid and certain in my hands.

I was dreaming about starlings the morning my parents' house burned down. That spring, a starling pair had begun building a nest in our attic. The vents to the attic weren't secured on all sides and the birds had swooped in through open corners, carrying twigs and bits of bark in their long, fine beaks. One afternoon, while they were out gathering materials, Stefan hammered down the vent edges to cut off their access. But when the birds returned, they managed to bully their way in, relentlessly pulling, pecking, and pushing against the wire. Once in the attic, they busied themselves weaving a home. But they couldn't fly out the way they'd flown in because of the twist in the wire. So we heard the insistent pinging of beak on metal as they tried to invent an exit. We could hear them flutter from one side of the attic to the other, tugging and clawing at each vent. Their organized inventory of escape routes became a frantic scratching and scrabbling as they realized they were trapped. They pounded their wings and clumsily beat themselves against the beams and rafters. Their calls became staccato and screeching; life was suddenly frenzied above our heads. We pried open one of the vents from the outside, but the starlings had become so panicked we couldn't tempt them out. They just kept flying in tighter circles, their soft, glossy bodies battering and bruising against the wood framing.

When things finally quieted down, Stefan went up to the attic to try to catch them. One bird was already dead; the other fluttered on the floor. He carried the survivor to the backyard, its heart throbbing in his palms at an impossible speed. He set it in the grass and we watched its chest rise and fall in hyperventilation, until a few moments later, in the shade of a rhododendron, it died. Almost immediately its feathers lost their gleam. As we dug a hole to bury the bird, Stefan said, "We have to fix the vents before more come."

The architect Grant Hildebrand writes that all species of animals, in their pursuit of protection from the elements and predators, seek shelters that have two characteristics in common—a sense of refuge and prospect, concepts originally explored by the British geographer Jay Appleton. As a refuge, a shelter is a small, dark space to carry out life's intimate rituals like feeding, resting, and procreating. But because animals cannot just conceal themselves and expect to survive, an ideal shelter provides guarded access to the expanse of the world—its prospect—where hunting, foraging, and courting are possible. In the formula for survival, refuge and prospect are opposites and necessary complements.

When it comes to survival in the wild, humans are at an evolutionary disadvantage. As a species we cannot run or climb with distinction; our senses of sight, hearing, and smell are utilitarian; we lack thick coats of fur, claws, and sharp teeth; we cannot fly. Our deficiencies underscore the primal importance of finding or erecting shelters that can adequately protect us. Hildebrand suggests that instincts influence our choice of where we live. We respond to elements of refuge and prospect in architecture and design—the way light plays in a space, the way a structure blends into a natural setting, the potential to retreat to quiet corners of a room, the view from a hill or a penthouse, the way landscaping defines public and private ground. Although we are tens of thousands of years removed from our ancestors' reliance on caves and grottos to provide protection from and access to nature, we still tap into the same instinctual behaviors.

I suspected the birds liked our house best because it was the tallest in the neighborhood. Stefan and I lived in a two-story ranch at the top of a hill. From the upstairs bedrooms we had a sweeping view of the neighborhood and its winding streets. When we buried the starling in the backyard, I considered our house for the first time in terms of its strategic vantage point—from the attic the birds must have been able to see even farther and better than we could from the second-story windows. High, dark, and cloistered, the attic was the perfect place to nest.

"Yes," I said, in answer to Stefan's comment. "More birds will come."

The thought of it worried me for weeks. I felt responsible for what had happened to the starlings, and the twinges of guilt carried into my dreams. The morning my parents' house burned down, fragments of waking life intruded on my sleep and, in the predawn dark, the distant wail of sirens became the distressed call of birds. The high-pitched avian cries grew loud and insistent until the ring of the telephone jarred me awake. Stefan rolled over to pick up the receiver. I wanted to slip back into sleep but drowsily listened to him as the birdcalls of my dreams morphed into the whine of fire engines navigating the hills around our house. At first Stefan spoke in a whisper, but then his voice came with loud alarm. He shook me, not realizing I was already half awake. I wanted to tell him that I had been dreaming about those poor birds we'd had in the attic a few months back, but before I could, he said, "Get up and get dressed. Your parents' house is on fire."

"My parents?"

"We've got to go now."

I fell out of bed and stumbled around the room looking for pants and socks. I felt useless, as though getting dressed was suddenly something new and terrifying. I crashed into Stefan as he came charging out of the closet pulling a T-shirt over his head. I threw on a jacket and raced out to the car with my sneakers in my hands. Friends were staying with us, so Stefan woke them to ask them to listen for our kids. As we drove on deserted, sleeping streets, I pictured my mother, a small but feisty eighty-year-old. Surely she'd heard the smoke alarm in time to get them out of the house safely. She had become a light sleeper in recent years while caring for my father, who had Alzheimer's. I thought about the locks we had installed on the inside of the house to keep my father from going out on his own. What if my mother hadn't been able to find the key, and they were trapped? I knitted my fingers together and rocked in the passenger seat. "Please, please let them be alright," I said in a low voice, trying to contain a panic rising up from my belly. I told myself that things were going to be fine, that my parents were going to be fine. I wanted to ask Stefan what he thought but was afraid of his honesty.

((

My mother had always dreamed of owning a house. She was the youngest of three children, born to Sarah and David, two eastern European Jews, who had come to the United States around the time of the First World War. Like many immigrants who settled in New York City, my grandparents first lived in cold-water flats on the Lower East Side and dreamed of having a bathroom they didn't have to share. After much hard work they eventually graduated to a rented railroad apartment in a four-story walk-up in Brooklyn. For Sarah and David, claiming space represented stability and status; home ownership proved they had successfully made it in the New World. The summer after my mother's sixth birthday, they bought a two-story Tudor row house in Laurelton, a Queens suburb of Manhattan. The house had been in foreclosure in the years following the stock market crash of 1929. That's how Sarah and David could afford to buy a house and why no one had the luxury of refusing to sell to Jews.

In a photo of my mother taken outside the Laurelton house, she stands flanked by her parents. Petite for her six years, she wears a pale, cotton yoke dress with an embroidered collar. She stares soberly into the camera, her strangely wistful expression symmetrically framed by a Buster Brown haircut. The photo was taken on a momentous day—moving day. Once when I asked her what she did the moment the shutter snapped, she said she didn't remember. Maybe she raced up the stairs to see her new room. Maybe she pushed through the boxes to see if her bike had been unloaded. Whatever she did after she flew away from the camera, it's doubtful she stopped to wonder whether the Laurelton house might be the last one she would live in. The row house outclassed the Brooklyn apartment, but as she got older, my mother set her sights on one day having a freestanding home; she fancied a space that didn't share an inside wall with another dwelling.

Growing up, it must have been impossible for my mother to imagine falling in love with a man who didn't share her sensibilities about owning a home. And yet, that's just what happened. In over fifty years of marriage, despite her persistent efforts to convince him otherwise, my father never showed the slightest interest in buying a house. On weekend trips to New England my parents repeated variations of the same conversation.

She: "Look at the gorgeous lawn at that place."

He: "You mean, look at how much work it is to mow."

She: "You can't deny it's lovely."

He: "Well, we can thank the poor slob who spent all week taking care of it."

It didn't matter if she pointed out the charm of a wraparound porch, the simplicity of a cottage silhouette, or the neighborliness of a late afternoon barbecue. All he saw was the opposite of convenience, anonymity, and options, which in his mind were the indisputable advantages of renting our apartment in Manhattan. On the surface, their disagreement appeared as a simple difference in preferences learned from childhood experiences, but at its heart was a conflict of instincts: my father didn't think he could survive in suburbia, and my mother thought the city was a place to visit, not settle down. In the hopes that he might someday change his mind, she collected clippings from decorating magazines in an idea book for feathering a future two-story nest.

When my father was growing up, his family moved from one apartment to another, taking advantage of Depression-era, "first month free" rental offers. That, he said, was how his mother saved enough money to keep food on the table. He described a good apartment as one that came with an upright piano, left behind by owners who had fallen on hard times and couldn't afford the expense of moving the instrument. Pianos were magnets for impromptu potluck parties, where everyone brought a little something to eat or drink or maybe just knew how to pound out a few tunes, something people could dance to and forget how poor they were. My father learned to value mobility, and although he and my mother lived for over three decades in the same Manhattan apartment, he knew that as renters they could flee and transform their lives at a moment's notice. But my mother had learned a different lesson from her immigrant parents, who considered home ownership proof they had the right to stay. These were the opposing forces that shaped my parents' sense of home. She wanted a place to permanently settle and call her own, and he wanted the freedom to bolt and leave everything behind. Understanding this difference gave deeper meaning to their terse arguments during our road trips through New England, which were not so much about specific houses but about how ingrained people's impulses can be about the nature and purpose of shelter.

(

Pumper and ladder trucks blocked the street. Yellow-clad fire-fighters moved quickly and decisively—manning hoses, wielding axes. I stepped around hoses and gear and moved through a small group of onlookers, their faces unfamiliar. My parents had just moved to town and I didn't know their neighbors yet. No one recognized us when Stefan and I arrived. In fact, no one was looking at us at all; their eyes were fixed on the sweep of orange flames racing across the roof of the house.

Thick black smoke poured out of the house's street-side windows; glass and smoldering debris were scattered across the lawn. The stink of burnt wood, fabric, paper, and plastic hung heavy in the air. The taste of family photos and antiques, keepsakes, and love letters settled as particulates on our lips. I rushed to the fire chief, who was directing his men via radio from his car. When I pleaded for my parents, he pointed to a house behind me while listening to a voice crackle over the airwave.

The couple next door had volunteered their home as a staging area and had been the ones who'd called us. Stefan and I arrived just in time to see my mother before she was transported to the hospital. She looked frail nested on the ambulance stretcher, her hair fanned out under her head, an oxygen mask peaked over her nose and mouth. I took her hand, crying. She nodded gently. "Smoke inhalation. No burns," the paramedic said, as he wheeled her away. "Her husband is inside."

I stepped into the neighbor's living room and found my father sitting in a hard-backed chair drinking juice and eating cookies from a plate on his lap. He seemed oblivious to the confusion around him. I put an arm over his shoulder and told him he was coming home with me. He asked if he could take the cookies with him, and the neighbors gave us the box.

My biggest fear driving back to my house was that my father was connected to the cause of the fire. He had suffered from Alzheimer's for over ten years and was at a stage in his illness when he restlessly tinkered and tampered with things—drapery cords, light-bulb sockets, cabinet latches. This inquisitive behavior had intensified since making the transition from the apartment in New York City to the Oregon house.

My parents had lived in their three-bedroom, twelfth-floor apartment for almost thirty-five years. It wasn't fancy or spacious, but like every other Manhattan apartment—shabby or chic—it offered retreat from the noise and crush of crowds on the street. My father used to instruct us that as soon as we left the apartment we had to look like we meant business, like we were in control, particularly when we felt confused or frightened. He called it wearing your "New York face." Early in his illness, he was still able to go out alone, moving through the streets with his usual steely aloofness. But then the street signs stopped making sense, and he wandered the neighborhood with a soft look of innocence, having forgotten why he'd left the apartment in the first place. My mother started taking him with her on her daily errands to make sure he got out, and for a long while he was her constant companion at the supermarket, pharmacy, and dry cleaners. But then he began to struggle with his balance and had to lean against her arm for each step. One day he stumbled while crossing at an intersection and, with traffic revving to go at the light, my mother had to enlist strangers to get him to his feet. The incident rattled her; it had become unsafe for him to walk outside. She leased a wheelchair to take him on strolls, but when he wouldn't stay in it, she abandoned the idea. The only choice left was to keep my father locked in the apartment. She didn't reach the decision lightly; it burdened her to reduce his world to the size of a few rooms, to transform his home from a place of refuge to one of captivity.

At first he was restless and insisted on leaving several times a day, but each time my mother distracted and redirected him. Still, he maintained a manic readiness to go somewhere. He paced the hallway outside his bedroom, jingling change in his pockets like he used to do when he walked to the subway on his way to work. He spent hours looking for his wallet, finding it, putting it away, forgetting where it was, and hunting for it all over again. He stood in front of the front door and puzzled over the key-entry locks we'd installed. One minute he'd demand to be let out and the next he'd scold that the door wasn't properly shut. But gradually he stopped asking to leave. Instead he spent hours watching people scurry through the streets, hovering twelve stories up like a bird of prey in a cage. This had gone on for two years before my mother and I considered whether she and my father could manage a move to the West Coast.

"Come out and buy a place near us and then I can help with Dad," I said to her one day on the phone. Stefan and I had just bought a house of our own.

"Can I do that?" she said.

I thought so but wasn't sure. Finally I said, "Of course."

That conversation revived my mother's childhood dreams. For months she talked about having a space where my father could get some fresh air—a fenced garden or patio. She retreated into memories of Laurelton, telling stories about the horse-drawn wagon deliveries of block ice for the icebox or describing the oak-lined streets that led to the local library. She recalled other houses, ones in Maine and Vermont that she had toured and fallen in love with, ones that looked out on gardens of wild flowers or cornfields. With each conversation she wondered out loud whether it was really possible to transplant her life and my father's to Oregon, and every time I said yes. Gradually, she started to believe it.

My mother couldn't leave my father long enough to house hunt, so I acted as her long-distance real estate proxy. The excitement of finding her dream home was quickly dampened by the criteria it needed to meet: it had to be laid out to protect my father from harming himself, within easy walking distance to shopping, and within my parents' fixed-income budget. I visited for-sale houses daily, sent her photos via email, and gave her virtual tours over the phone. The house they finally purchased met all of the necessary conditions but lacked any charm. It was a sturdy 1950s ranch with a wraparound garden. The outside was nice enough, but the interior was a retro hodgepodge of colors and styles. The kitchen was painted shiny institutional beige with sky-blue Formica countertops and faux leaded glass cabinet doors. The main bathroom had a 1970s orange sink and was accented in dark oak trim. Every room had matted taupe carpeting and out-of-use electric baseboard heaters. Compared to the Colonial Revival and Cape Cod cottage homes my mother admired, this place wasn't much more than floor, walls, and fixtures; it didn't come close to the house she'd always dreamed of. And because the inspection report revealed that the roof needed repair, she wouldn't have any extra money to redecorate. "Let's take it," she said one evening over the phone. She spoke with the resolve of a person who knew that her only chance was also her last chance.

Although we didn't talk about it openly, both my mother and I knew that if my father's dementia hadn't been as advanced as it was, he never would have agreed to move. Alzheimer's had stripped his impulses about place and its importance; he couldn't remember that he had only ever wanted to live in an apartment in the city. As my mother sorted and packed a lifetime's worth of belongings and furnishings, he circled around her and wondered aloud what was happening. She told him they were going on vacation, doing spring-cleaning, or whatever came to mind. Sometimes she risked telling him they'd bought a house, and were leaving and never coming back. Each time, he reacted with surprise, immediately forgot to care, and then, a few minutes later, returned to ask again. Because this kind of repetition was characteristic of his illness, it didn't stand out to my mother as unusual when he inquired over and over, "Are we going somewhere?" But it's impossible to say whether or not his question was in fact rooted in his primal brain, guiding his most basic instincts and his deepest desire to stay where he was.

A few days after the fire, I received a call to meet with the fire inspector and the insurance adjuster. I worried that the damages wouldn't be covered if they thought my father had played a role in causing them. I met the two men at the ruin of the house.

"Your parents were very lucky," the fire inspector said, steering me around a section of the ceiling that had collapsed by the front door. "This was a really hot fire."

My heartbeat filled my ears as I tried to calm the image of my parents panicking in the inferno. I stood next to the open front door and absentmindedly fiddled with the inside locks we'd installed. How did my mother have the presence of mind to get them both out, fumbling with keys in all that smoke and heat? Did she notice that the light switches had begun to melt to the walls? Was she aware that the living room windows were about to explode? I could feel how my mother's hands must have shaken as she struggled with the keys in the door. I felt dizzy standing in the charred debris and leaned against the wall, its shape distorted from the heat.

The fire inspector estimated that my parents had no more than two minutes from the time they exited until the flames rolled across the ceiling, at which point any hope of escape or rescue would have been impossible. He traced the start of the blaze to a couch pushed up against an old baseboard heater. We thought the heaters had been disconnected before my parents moved in, but one mistakenly had been left on a live circuit attached to an old thermostat. I guessed that my father had fiddled with the dial and turned the thermostat on.

"We wondered about all the locks," the insurance adjuster said, speaking up for the first time.

I stood very still. We even had locks on the doors leading to the kitchen and garage to keep my father away from the stove and furnace.

"Your mother seems very capable," the insurance adjuster said. "Does your father have any disability?"

I didn't answer at first, pulling my lips in. What if the insurance policy was void because of my father's Alzheimer's? What would we do if my parents lost their equity in the house? I didn't know whether to lie or not. The door was open behind me, but I felt trapped.

"You can tell us," the insurance adjuster said, reassuringly. "We only disqualify claims in cases of arson, and this clearly was not arson."

I let my jaw relax and took a small step toward the two men. The blackened walls of the room seemed to widen, making space enough to bring the whole story to light.

❨

For the next eight months, a reclamation company rebuilt and remodeled every inch of my parents' eighteen-hundred-square-foot home. The interior walls, surfaces, and appliances were removed until the house was reduced to studs and siding. As the work was just getting underway, the construction foreman called my mother and me to the site to look at flooring samples. From the porch you could still take in the pungent stink of smoke soaked into the wood framing. It triggered a visceral flashback of heat and confusion, and my mother couldn't take a step past the front door. She turned and headed for the driveway, saying I should pick out the flooring without her. Later, I found her sitting in my car, staring blankly at the soot-smeared garage doors.

"This is all my fault," she said. "He never wanted a house."

Growing up in our Manhattan apartment, I had inherited my mother's dreams of picket fences and gabled roofs. Silent in the back seat of the car on our family drives through Connecticut, Massachusetts, and Maine, I had favored her sensibility, not my father's, and tried to picture myself in the homes that sailed past the window. That sense of place deepened when I moved from big cities to small towns and walked through neighborhoods with houses nested in rows. I saw those houses as more than just shells to occupy; each one had a story to tell about how it had come to be, and why it was suited to some people and not others. In that vulnerable moment sitting in the driveway, I had to make my mother see that her instincts to buy this house had been right, that its story was meant to be her story, that a person's sense of home is an intricate combination of desire and destiny. My mother wasn't a religious person but believed that everything happens for a reason, that there is meaning in each moment of our lives. Sitting beside her in the car, I realized that I had to make her see that the mounting signs—the ones she considered bad omens—pointed to good fortune.

"The house knew," I said. "It knew it wasn't your dream house."

I spoke with urgency. There was no going back to the East Coast; all of my parents' finances were tied up in the Oregon house. If my mother doubted her decision to move west, she might never alight and settle down. It is a crippled existence to spend your life wondering whether or not you've made the wrong choice. I knew that I needed to make her understand that this house—and no other—was meant to be hers. Like my mother, I was also a believer of signs, but I had come to consider the fire as a ghastly kind of good luck. I made a mental list of the fortunate string of misfortunes that had led us to sit parked in a blackened driveway: the unavoidable nature of my father's illness had allowed my mother to give herself permission to purchase the house; the debilitating loss of his memory meant he couldn't remember to fight the decision to move; the mortgage brokers' unscrupulous lending practices, which would ultimately lead to the crash of the housing market, allowed my mother to buy property with my father's money but without his consent; and finally, with the house's total destruction and the generous insurance claim, she now had the chance to build her dream home. But I sensed she wasn't strong enough to accept the stark truth of such a list; so I told her a story instead.

"We had a friend," I said. "Her name was Barb and she lived in a ranch, kind of like yours, but it was tucked into the hills."

I remembered Barb's house well. It was a cedar construction with a wraparound porch under a canopy of trees. Barb had spent years remodeling the place, and when she divorced, she fought to keep it. Although she got the house as part of the settlement, it became a bitter reminder of an unsuccessful marriage. She ended up leaving town and selling it.

"A few days after the sale closed," I said, "and a week before the new owner moved in, the house burned to the ground."

My mother turned to me with an earnest look.

"They thought the deck was struck by lightning. But they never knew for sure."

When I heard the news that Barb's house had burned, it immediately made sense to me.

The house had defined the literal and figurative shape of Barb's sorrow for so many years that I wasn't surprised when it went up in flames. It was as if the house had known it could no longer serve as a shelter for someone else and surrendered in a finale of superheated exhaustion.

"So, you don't think it was a mistake that I bought the house?" my mother said.

"No, Mom, I think the fire was a sign that you deserve your dream house."

Turning points often reduce to binary decisions: fight or flee, adapt or resist, doubt or believe. I watched my mother calculate her options. She let herself settle into the passenger seat, her back and shoulders folding into the upholstery. She clasped her hands across her lap. She took a deep breath. She turned to me with tired, resolute eyes. And then, in a flat tone, she asked me about the flooring samples. I told her everything I'd learned about laminates, and when there was nothing left to say, she asked me to remind her to ask the contractor about the cost of installing hardwood floors. And just like that, she signaled her decision to stay.

The contractors coated the studs with shellac and closed the walls, and as the smell of the fire faded from the structure, my mother finally felt comfortable going to see the progress of the work. She picked out new tiles, countertop surfaces, trims, and color schemes. She debated appliances, drawer pulls, cabinetry, and window coverings. With the money the reclamation company saved by replacing the plaster and lathe with gypsum board, the insurance company let her reinvest the difference in new windows, an architectural roof, and hardwood floors. Month by month, room by room, the house became a charming space. It turned into everything she had always dreamed of.

For eight months my mother and father lived in my home while theirs was rebuilt. We counted down the days, waiting for the final touches to be done. It felt like a lifetime had gone by with the seasons. Before long, the starlings filled the skies again, looking for places to nest. Stefan made sure our attic was secure this time. Then, with just a week to go before the move-in date, my father died in his sleep. Moving day was as somber as it was auspicious. My mother carried my father's ashes in a ceramic urn across the threshold of her brand new house. Without any furnishings, our voices ricocheted off the walls and windows. We spoke softly and explored quietly, as if we had broken into a church. Unlike when she was six years old, no one suggested taking a picture of my mother; no one was interested in documenting the veil of vulnerability shrouding her face the first time she opened the door onto those echoing rooms. I watched her timidly inspect the empty closets and cabinets, as though hoping to find something that belonged to her, some sign that she was meant to be there.

When my mother stood in the doorway to the kitchen, the light streamed in from the windows behind her, and I pictured her preparing dinner next to the sink, chopping onions and humming along with the radio. I imagined her recipe collection scattered across the dining table and the savory scent of sautéed garlic and herbs filling the air. I could see her wipe her hands on her apron and take a moment to look out into the garden. The view of her dahlias, roses, and sunflowers might prompt her to tell the story about her mother's Polish gardener, who had used to threaten that gypsies would steal and eat the family dog as punishment for digging in the flowerbeds. I imagined my mother laughing as she told the story. Standing with her now in the kitchen of her empty home, I hoped she felt what I was feeling—that even though we hadn't moved in any of her dishes, furniture, books, or bedding, the house had already begun to fill.

When my niece, Maya, called for the third time in three weeks, she wanted to know what the hell was going on over there, and by over there she meant Oregon, where, I said, I was up a tree. And by up a tree I didn't mean in some kind of trouble with money or my marriage, which she might have understood, but actually on a ladder in a tree, a concept harder for her to wrap her head around.

"It's canning season," I said, hoping that would explain every-thing.

Like me, Maya was born and raised in Manhattan and now lived in the West. While I had followed a sense of adventure to Oregon, she had followed the love of her life to Montana. When she called, I had been living in the Willamette Valley for ten years, a decade during which I had developed unhurried talents like gardening and bread baking. But Maya had only recently settled in Missoula, and her ties to city living were still urgent and crackling. In Big Sky Country, life had grown small quickly, the way it does in western towns that are a refuge in the wild. With a view of the Bitterroot Mountains out her back door, I hoped she would learn lessons of seasonality from the landscape. This, I thought, might help her better understand my push to bring in my late summer fruit. But as a fresh transplant to the West, she wore rural living the way you wear someone else's clothes—with reservation and self-consciousness. It made her edgy in her new environment. I heard irritation in her voice.

"Which tree is it this time?"

"Pear."

"And last time?"

"Plum."

She could have said "And the time before that?" but she didn't because, I think, she knew that hearing my long list of seasonal preserved foods would exhaust her patience. She had called to talk about her upcoming wedding, which is what she had called about the last two times I was up a tree. I had considered letting the phone ring through to voicemail, but in our family we always make time to talk even if it's to say we don't have time to talk. I would have liked to have climbed down from the ladder, taken a seat in the shade, and weighed the details of her dress and veil, but like every seasonal canner, I was preoccupied with the urgency of rot. From the moment we pluck, down, or reel in our food, microorganisms in the air, soil, and water initiate a process of deterioration. Life force is nature's most potent preservative. End it, and our fruits, vegetables, and meat begin to spoil. As I listened to Maya describe her options for wedding locations, I stared into the bucket with the dozen pears I'd collected so far. The problem wasn't that they'd rot before my eyes but that they were in a queue of other already-picked foods that were slowly, imperceptibly going bad in boxes in my garage. With all of that produce waiting, my days unfolded like a series of conditional statements. If I brought in the pears today, then I could pickle the green beans I'd harvested yesterday. If I finished my pickling by tomorrow, then I could pick basil for the first batches of pesto. If I could bag and freeze the pesto by the weekend, then I could can the pears after they'd sweetened for a week off the tree. And if everything went according to plan, I'd have time for tomatoes, corn, broccoli, and late-season berries, and then could start all over with another round. But if I waited too long for any of it, something or everything would spoil. I had no time to waste.

"I wish I could talk," I said, shifting my weight on the ladder, the rungs pressing into the arches of my feet.

"When will you be done?"

It seemed unbelievable to admit that I would be occupied with picking and putting up food for the next four weeks, even though that was when I expected to have sealed the last jars of applesauce and salsa.

"Soon," I said. "Soon."

If I could have read my niece's thoughts, I might have heard her ask, "Why waste your time? Why not just go to the store?" These were questions I sometimes asked myself after scalding my fingers while submerging hot jars into boiling pots of water during late-night canning sessions, alone with only steam for company. Was the effort really worth it? I once calculated the savings in dollars and cents. The outcome was favorable until I put a price on the time spent in the orchard, the garden, and the kitchen. And there is little doubt that it is more convenient to buy two dozen jars of blackberry jam than it is to fight through the thickets of thorns to collect berries for a homemade batch. And so, when anyone questions my decision to can for weeks on end, it's difficult to describe, let alone quantify, the sense of satisfaction associated with producing your own food. How do you measure the pleasure of opening the cupboard and seeing rows of jars labeled in your own handwriting, gleaming in deep shades of purple, red, gold, and green? Because it was not something I grew up doing, it's especially difficult to explain to my family. Where would my mother even have stored a canning pot in the narrow cabinets in our apartment's galley kitchen?

After ten years of putting up my own food, I've realized that I won't find the true value of canning in my bank account. I find it in my garden, in the garden of my grandmother, and in the gardens of her foremothers where, for millennia, what's ripe for the picking has spoken to our most basic survival instincts: the body starves when the season's bounty withers on the vine.

(

Canning is a modern convention that was introduced around the turn of the nineteenth century, but food preservation is ancient. As early as 12,000 BCE, Middle Eastern tribes dried fish and other foods in the desert sun. Today, we associate preserved food with its relationship to cultural tastes—fermented kimchi is as emblematic of Korea as salted prosciutto is of Italy. But long before it was a characteristic of cuisine, preserved food played an important historical role that shaped not just what we eat but also how we live. Around 9000 BCE the first farmers planted and sowed wheat and barley. Three thousand years later, the introduction of the plow and irrigation made it possible to expand small-scale farms to large plots. With the ability to produce food in sufficient amounts, our ancestors no longer needed to roam to collect plants and roots, and they gave up their nomadic, hunter-gatherer existence to establish agrarian societies. By producing food in large quantities, they met their immediate needs and had surplus to store for future consumption. The trick was devising storage methods that prevented food from rotting. Once they figured out how to dry, salt, ferment, and smoke goods, they could settle in one place and survive the seasons when food was scarce. Over time, the practicality of putting up food extended beyond an individual's survival, and people preserved enough staples to give as gifts and sell at market, opening up avenues for community and commerce. I keep a favorite plum sauce recipe, stained and creased, pressed between the pages of my canning cookbook; it is tailored to the specific variety of tart plums that grow in my garden. Handling it makes it easy to imagine how, for thousands of years, families must have passed down their own time-tested recipes. Friends, neighbors, and relatives must have come to know one another by the food they produced and put up. I don't doubt they passed their recipes down to new generations with the same pride and care with which they told their ancestral stories, because the truth about our past goes hand in hand with the secrets of sustaining ourselves in the future.

In her book on the art and science of food preservation, Sue Shephard explains that preserved food made it possible for our ancestors to settle down but also to venture forth. Like never before, they could travel long distances—by land and sea—across unfamiliar territories, where food was potentially unavailable. Preserved food could keep for long periods on boats and horseback, in extremes of hot and cold; it was often compact in size and concentrated in nutrition. Around 2500 BCE, Polynesians carried fermented breadfruit and dried sweet potatoes when they crossed thousands of miles of open water in canoes to establish new settlements in the Pacific Ocean. In the fifth century BCE, Herodotus, the Greek historian, journeyed through the Near East to learn the customs of other cultures and very likely traveled with cured olives and grape leaves set in brine. And the extended sea voyages of explorers like Ferdinand Magellan and Vasco de Gama—with land and the promise of fresh provisions nowhere on the horizon—would have been unthinkable without salted meat and hardtack.

The feats of exploration made possible by preserved food are, however, a study in contrasts. The smoked and dried staples that fed curious explorers also nourished invaders. Napoleon is credited with saying, "An army marches on its stomach," a truism; preserved food is essential for foreign conquest. During the Napoleonic Wars, the French government, eager to find a way to feed its ranks of soldiers, promised twelve thousand francs to the inventor who developed a method for inexpensively preserving large quantities of food. In 1809, a French confectioner and brewer named Nicolas Appert discovered that when food is cooked inside sealed glass jars it does not spoil unless the seal breaks or leaks. Appert was correct in his observations and the canning tradition was born. Appert couldn't explain why this method worked; scientific understanding of the role of microbes and bacteria in food spoilage was still half a century away. But the absence of explanation did not prevent the mass production of preserved foods—first in glass and then, a few years later, in tins. The utility and necessity of preserved food was recognized not only by explorers and invaders, however. Invaders arrived in new lands and encountered people who had their own stockpiles of local delicacies. Seeing the approach of unfamiliar regiments, ships, and caravans, the indigenous populations of the world must have weighed the same question: Do we share what we have in friendship or stash our reserves in case of war? Whatever the answer, throughout history, preserved food has helped people embrace and endure the unexpected.

It is impossible for me to identify the precise moment when my seasonal preoccupation with canning began, but I suspect it had to do with the thirty days I spent backpacking in the Colorado Rockies with Outward Bound. Each week, my group had to carry everything we needed to eat for seven days, with no chance of more until our next resupply. There were eight of us in the group, each of us loaded with sixty to seventy pounds of gear and staples. The food we carried was familiar—flour and yeast; dried nuts and raisins; pasta and salt; rice and freeze-dried beans; "fat crackers" made with generous amounts of butter and sugar. What was unfamiliar, however, was why we carried these things and not others. As a city girl who had never spent time in the backcountry, I didn't immediately understand that we needed enough daily calories to keep up our strength and that the components of those calories should be compact and long-lasting; I had never calculated using this formula before. Moving through the peaks, spines, and drainages of the Grenadier Range, perishables like meat, bread, fresh fruits and vegetables would have been impractical because there was no room in our packs for anything that might spoil. Rotten food was inedible; inedible food was waste; and waste had to be packed out because of our commitment to "leave no trace." In the mountains, carrying around garbage is a poor use of the muscle mass and body fat you need to stay fit and warm while hiking into a cold headwind. I didn't give much thought to how my experience in the Rockies faintly mirrored that of the pioneers, explorers, and nomads who had rationed out their concentrated, dried, and fermented foodstuffs. I didn't consider this trip a harbinger for lessons about the connection between food, preservation, and survival. Most of the time all I thought about was how to keep my blistered, bleeding feet from getting infected. And the rest of the time I tried to ignore that I was almost always hungry.

Shortly after my wilderness experience, I left the familiarity of East Coast, big-city living and moved first to Portland, Oregon, and then to a college town on the banks of the Willamette River. It was here, in an agricultural community, that I gradually began to recognize the seasonal cycle of food. While I'd known all along that food doesn't come from the grocery store, it was in Oregon that I learned about the narrow margins that separate a successful harvest from fear of famine. I met and married Stefan, an agricultural scientist, and his deep concerns about plowing, sowing, and harvesting revealed a purposeful preoccupation with soil temperature, weekly rainfall, and degree days. I learned that a ten-minute hailstorm in May can wreck a season's cherry crop. Putting corn in the ground a week too late can threaten the yield. Ignoring the life cycle of leaf-eating beetles can mean plowing a field under and calling it quits until the following year. It was in this atmosphere of ecological vigilance that the local residents tended robust backyard gardens

own peril. As a kid, I remember looking up botulism in the *World Book Encyclopedia*; the descriptions of progressive paralysis held fast and, three decades later, made me nervous when I started canning on my own. It took two seasons of helping other people put up their pickles and salsas until I had the confidence to go solo. The first time I worked alone in my kitchen, I canned a few small batches of applesauce. It wasn't the fun time I'd had when I'd canned with friends; I fretted over my jars, worried that they wouldn't seal. After pulling them from the hot water bath, I stared at them and waited to witness the vacuum drawing the lid down, making each jar "ping." I worried so much about having done something wrong that I wouldn't let my children sample any of my canned goods until I had shelved them for weeks, tasted them myself, and waited a day or two to prove they weren't contaminated.

But with each passing year, as my family survived my batches of sauces and jams, I developed more self-confidence and expanded my repertoire with compotes and salsas. When I wanted to add more variety, I traded fruit from my trees for vegetables from other people's gardens, and started putting up pickles and whole tomatoes. I went to bed most nights in the early fall listening for the telltale pinging of jars in the kitchen and woke to a row of edible jewels on my countertop. Whenever I gave my mother any of my homemade goods, she would run a hand around the metal ring of the jars before putting them in the refrigerator. I tried to explain to her that they didn't need to be refrigerated until after they were opened, but she was unmoved by this. She would smile and set them on the shelf next to the butter and eggs. For all I knew, she emptied the jars into the sink after I left, worried that they had already gone bad.

My experience in my modern kitchen is not so unlike that of the first farmers—all of us operating with a degree of ignorance and faith. From Africa to South America, China to India, early agrarians knew that certain techniques for preserving food worked. They didn't know why their methods worked, but that didn't dampen their ambitions. With no knowledge of microorganisms, they relied on their powers of observation. Through experimentation they could see that meat and fish set out on hot sand and sunbaked stones would keep for weeks, as would catches and kills hung in dry breezes and over smoking fires. They didn't know they were eliminating the conditions that promote rotting; they didn't know that the microorganisms that decompose food generally prefer a warm, moist, slightly acidic environment to grow. Likewise, they didn't understand why the bacteria in milk and yeasts were favorable for making cheese, yogurt, beer, and wine; they only knew they had found a way to extend the use of dairy, grain, and fruit products that would have otherwise spoiled with time.

This is on my mind when my daughter helps me with the jamming and wants to know why the air in the headspace of the jars doesn't have "germs" in it. When I learned to can, no one ever explained the science associated with each step of the process. Unable to explain the physics of a vacuum, I tell my daughter what I have been told: if you pack hot fruit in hot, sterile jars and boil them, you get a good seal. I hand down my techniques the way they were passed down thousands of years ago—with the earnest acceptance of a truth that I am unable to justify. In 1675, when Antony van Leeuwenhoek first observed "animalcules," or microorganisms, through his handmade microscope, the discovery could not dispel the belief that putrefaction was a mysterious, spontaneous process. It would take nearly another two hundred years for Louis Pasteur to definitively document that airborne microorganisms are responsible for food spoilage. By then, the cultures of the world had long-standing traditions of putting up food. They neither awaited nor needed any reasons for why their methods worked.

Up a tree in my garden, I understand my niece's impatience with my canning, especially given how easy it is to take for granted the role preserved foods play in our day-to-day lives. We forget how much we rely on them, but a quick inventory of the average kitchen tells an old story. Anyone with a refrigerator or freezer channels the Inuit logic of preserving seal meat and fish in snow caves. Anyone who snacks on trail mix enjoys a salty-sweetness reminiscent of the dried meat and fruits that Native Americans used to make pemmican. It is easy to forget that the rice, millet, lentils, split peas, oats, and popcorn in our cupboards are processed as dry goods, and that that process has been used for thousands of years to ensure staples are readily available. For centuries, in the high elevations of the Andes Mountains, Incan farmers set out potatoes on successive cold nights and stomped on the frozen tubers, using an early freeze-drying technique that eventually evolved into a food preparation method that would nourish astronauts in space. Cheese, cured cold cuts, canned tuna, frozen concentrated orange juice, and pickles are only a few of the things we eat every day that are prepared and packaged to keep. And it's not just what we eat, but also the value we place on preserved food, particularly in times of crisis. At the first sign of blizzards and hurricanes, people stock up, clearing supermarket shelves of tinned and vacuum-packed goods. In the hours before a big storm, standing in line with a shopping cart full of goods to see us through the hard times, we are doing what our ancestors have done for thousands of years.

After hanging up with my niece, I slipped my cell phone into my pocket and took a step higher on my ladder. I braced myself with one hand, and stretched up to reach the heavy, high-hanging pears. The ladder wobbled on the uneven ground, and my heart skipped a beat. It would be like this all day, spikes of adrenaline as I reached and leaned to strip the tree. In all my years of canning, I have never fallen off the ladder, but the near misses always conjure the same question: What am I doing up here? Although the answer is reflected in the lives of the ancients, I really need only look as far back as my childhood. Growing up, one of my greatest fears was getting trapped in the elevator of our apartment building. I knew from what I'd seen on television and in the movies that bad things happen in stuck elevators—people die, disappear, and even drown. The handful of times I got stuck, I immediately began a quiet calculation: How long can I survive in here? The only times I could completely let down my guard and ride the twelve flights up to the apartment without anxiety were on Friday evenings when, after doing the weekly grocery shopping with my mother, we had bags filled with food. I knew on those nights that if we got stuck in the elevator for days or weeks—the way it sometimes happened in my nightmares—we'd have enough supplies to wait for a rescue. That, I thought, was canning's real hold on me, a childhood desire to be stocked up and ready for anything. The neat rows of fruits and vegetables in my cupboard give me the same feeling of safety that my mother's overstuffed shopping bags did.

I thought my niece might relate more to my memories of riding my apartment building elevator than anything I might tell her about our enduring bond with the ancient farmers who salted, dried, and candied their harvests. After all, growing up in New York City, she had been stuck in her share of elevators. I decided to tell her this in a few weeks, when my last jars were sealed and I finally got around to calling her back. I repeated her words in my head, "What the hell is going on over there?" It must have seemed to her that I had traveled far from city life, from what she knew, from home. But for me canning was a kind of return, not a departure, a journey a few steps beyond the supermarket into the landscape of survival, where we all live. It can be hard to put that kind of sentiment into words over the phone when high-hanging fruit or pots of simmering sauce demand immediate attention. Really, I thought, I would do better to send her a jar of homemade jam. It speaks for itself.

((Blue Means Water

When you grow up on an island, you can circumnavigate the limits of your world by following a forever-arcing line. There are different names for different kinds of islands, names like *islets* or *keys*. An island in a river is sometimes called an *eyot* or an *ait*, words I have never seen written on any map. We didn't have a special name for where we lived; I didn't know there could be a special name for it. We just called it the city. And although the city, Manhattan, is an island bounded by three rivers, I never thought about being surrounded on all sides by water; the lines of my world were drawn at right angles, a march of intersecting rows of buildings. Standing on a corner, facing off with a crowd on the opposite side of the street and waiting for the light to change, everyone had their eyes fixed forward, edgy to advance. No one ever seemed concerned that if they went too long in one direction, eventually they might cast themselves into the murky depths of the Hudson, East, or Harlem Rivers. We weren't those kinds of islanders; this wasn't that kind of island.

Our three-bedroom, twelfth-floor apartment was on the lower west side. From the two smaller bedrooms there was an interrupted view of the Hudson. Between a post office parking lot and a public housing complex, we could see the river flow in the background and watch the sun sink into New Jersey, folding thick lines of pink and orange down into a distant, darkening cityscape on the horizon. Ships of all kinds—cruise lines, tug boats, and garbage barges—made their way up and down the water. During Fleet Week, guided missile destroyers and historic naval tall ships drifted past. When my brothers saw a big boat, they would call me, and we would sit on the windowsill and measure the vessel's size relative to the warehouses on the riverfront. This was the view I was accustomed to, the water as a reference point for the city. When, for my ninth birthday, a family friend took me on a Circle Line cruise around the tip of Manhattan, the sight of the city from the water was disquieting because the usual relationship of foreground and background had shifted. Although I'd lived on an island all my nine years, for the first time I felt surrounded by water. "Look, look," the family friend said. "You can see your building from here." This, I thought, is what it must feel like to be kidnapped by pirates. "What am I doing out here," I wondered, "when I belong over there?" It was the only time I sailed around the city. Once was enough.

A bird's eye view of New York City appears to be a near-perfect lattice. This makes navigating the streets an arithmetic exercise. When looking for an address, the question is always simple: Are the numbers going up or down? Of course there are exceptions, particularly at the tip of the island, where the first settlers and merchants arranged the streets on diagonals. But get above the city—by flying over or looking down from a tall building—and the lasting impression is of uniform, intersecting lines. My sense of east and west was practical. I knew that the sun rises in the east and sets in the west, and boiled down this truism to its most essential fact: if I faced the entrance to our apartment building, the promise of popsicle-colored dusks over the Hudson was in front of me. Somewhere behind me was another river with a view of the rising sun. But I never went over there; I didn't know that neighborhood.

I still make my way in the world by turning my body to face the things that matter most to me. This struck me as a good a way as any to navigate, but it is not for everyone. The first time my father-in-law, Klaus, visited Stefan and me in Oregon, he wanted to know about the rivers that run through our town. I told him there are two—the Marys and the Willamette. Klaus quickly narrowed his inquiry: What were the rivers' sources and points of confluence? I swung my arm in a rough sweep behind me to indicate, with no precision whatsoever, that somewhere out there they flowed in some direction of which I was not aware. It was difficult to tell whether I saw disbelief or disappointment in my father-in-law's face. Looking back, I suspect it was both.

I referred him to Stefan, saying, "He'll know."

"Yes, I'm sure he will," said Klaus, who had made basic orienteering a staple of his sons' upbringing.

It makes sense that my father-in-law would be curious about the rivers—and about other things like the birdsongs, rates of rainfall, and summit elevations—that characterized our section of the state. As a retired geography teacher, his vocation demanded a focus on the features of the land—where it rises, falls, and cedes to water. But over time, I learned that his real interest in the Willamette and the Marys was more fundamental than any training he had had for a career in the classroom. Klaus is most at home in the woods. On his parcel of land in southern Germany he fells trees for winter heating and hikes in the dense understory of the Black Forest to collect mushrooms. He can tell the time by the angle of the sun in a particular season; he can predict weather patterns by the direction of the wind. As a child he learned to catch trout with his bare hands in the stream that ran outside his village, and in the lean years after the Second World War, his fishing helped feed his family. For him, nature was not an abstract idea; it was an essential constant. So when he orients himself via the landscape, it tells him not just where he is but where he needs to be. When he showed me on a map the positions and paths of the Willamette and the Marys, it was with the tenderness of sharing a gift; he explained how they define the southern and eastern borders of our town, and how he would never struggle to find his way to and from our apartment now that he knew the rivers' locations. I picked up the map and turned it to the direction I was facing. This was also how I navigated in the car, swiveling the map to read it as if the world was always straight ahead of me. My sense of orientation is tactile; I need landmarks to define where I am and where I'm headed. So as Klaus talked about east and west, I made mental notes: when facing my apartment, the Willamette was to my left (in the direction of the supermarket and the highway on-ramp) and the Marys was in front of me (toward the park I never visited and didn't know the name of). Klaus now knew where the apartment was, based on the rivers' paths, and I now knew the rivers' positions based on the apartment's location. We'd both learned something, but neither changed how we navigated our way home.

"You know that the sun rises in the east and sets in the west," Klaus asked, with no malice in his voice.

"Yes," I said. "I know."

Growing up in New York City, if I walked four long blocks down our street in the direction of the setting sun I would come to the Hudson River. But I never did that, go to the river, because the industrial strip was a red-light district and the Westside Highway blocked access to the water. The water, I'd heard, was swift-moving and contaminated. "If you fall in," a friend once said to me, "keep your mouth shut or you might swallow garbage." They said anyone who fell in the Hudson automatically received a tetanus shot if they went to the hospital, no matter when you had your last booster. The time I was treated to the Circle Line ride around Manhattan, I worried about inhaling any of the spray kicked up by the wind, thinking that a hypodermic needle was waiting for me when we docked. The river did have one draw, however. Once a year, we went to Battery Park to watch the Fourth of July fireworks shot from barges in the bay where the Hudson and East Rivers flow into each other. This was the water's most important role for me—a glassy backdrop to a choreographed display of light.

When you look at a map of New York City it is easy to trace a blue line of water around the perimeter. If nature played a bigger role in the city's landscape, then the river might have captured more of my attention. But the fact that I was surrounded on all sides by water seemed a technicality in the city's geography. Before we got married, Stefan visited my family for the first time. He got turned around every time we emerged from the subway. He'd learned from his father to look up and put the passing landscape in perspective to create an internal map. When they hiked as a family in the Alps, moving at a human rate of speed, it was easy to keep the horn of a peak or the meander of a river in sight as constant points of reference. But after traveling underground for a mile or more and emerging suddenly from the dark, navigational landmarks disappear. It's not that the universal constants that anchor us to the poles are irrelevant in a city like New York; it's just that they seem inconsequential.

"This way," I'd say, after rounding the bend at the top of the subway staircase.

"Is that south?" Stefan would say.

"It's downtown."

Today, not far from where I grew up, in a neighborhood we never explored as children, is the High Line, a park built on an old rail line that is elevated thirty feet above the city streets. Running along the city's west side, it is only two avenue blocks from the Hudson River. When I meet friends there to give them a tour of the city, we stand with our backs to the water as I point out the landmarks from my childhood—where my parents lived, the black-top park in the Meatpacking District where my softball team had practice, the first apartment I rented with a friend after college. Rarely do I think to turn around and admire the water. When we do, I don't have much to say about what we see.

"Maybe if the Hudson flowed through the city and not around it," I said to Stefan, who wondered why I never suggested we go down to the river. "Maybe I'd be more interested," I said, "if it were more in the way." After he asked several times, we decided to ride the commuter ferry to and from Staten Island, just to get out on the water. The whole time my eyes were fixed on the cityscape, but Stefan noticed how the curve of the island is defined where the Hudson and East Rivers come together to form Manhattan Bay. He asked questions that would echo years later in my conversation with Klaus—questions about the source and history of these two bodies of water that define the edges of the city.

In contrast to Klaus's visit, when my father came to see Stefan and me for the first time in Oregon, he told me that as long as he could see the county courthouse steeple or find the downtown Dairy Mart, he could find his way back to our apartment. Like me, he'd grown up on the criss-cross of New York City's streets and avenues. Because you can't see the county courthouse steeple or the Dairy Mart from everywhere in town, Stefan tried to draw my father's attention to the difference between the Cascade Mountains (to the east) and the Coast Range (to the west), both of which are visible on a clear day from almost wherever you are. Like New York City, our town is mostly organized on a grid, except only some of the streets are in numerical order while the others are named after United States presidents in historical order. My father didn't seem to pay attention to Stefan's brief geography lesson and joked about not having enough time to brush up on his American history to keep from getting lost. Really, I thought he was talking to me in code, from one New Yorker to another, saying, "Sugar, what are you doing here?" I detected a note of betrayal in his voice, as if being in the West went against everything he had expected of and hoped for me. Or maybe he just missed me, living three thousand miles away. In that moment, I doubt that either of us could have predicted the direction my life was headed or how living in that small town, sandwiched between mountains and bounded by rivers, would take me further away from my childhood home than could be measured in miles. My father flew back to New York City and never visited again before he moved here with my mother. Meanwhile, I inched forward in this new landscape and, for the first time in my life, started to try to make sense of the world using a map.

((

The car is littered with maps. They are everywhere—folded into side pockets, sandwiched between seats, crumpled underfoot. Each has a purpose, tells a story. But none is perfect, nor ever can be. Maybe that's why Stefan and I collect them the way we do whenever we are on the road, piecing them together like a two-dimensional puzzle to decode the three-dimensional world speeding past us. To reconcile what we see out of the window with what is printed on the page, we rely on a consistent set of cues—green means forest, brown means desert, blue means water.

I trace the blue lines in the road atlas, heading south on Highway 395 through northeastern California, and stop my finger on Mono Lake. I know it will be too cold to swim this time of year, but just the idea of it—shimmering in the thin light of early spring—is too inviting to pass up. Because of that, and the fact that it is on our way, we decide to stop. When we arrive, the melting March snow makes it difficult to pick a path to the shoreline without soaking our sneakers, but our children are determined to get as close to the water as possible. They consider how best to navigate their way to the shore by balancing on scattered rocks, exposed and glistening in the sun. I see what they choose to ignore, that the trail of rocks disappears beneath a blanket of snow a few yards from where we are standing. But they are full of solutions, and take off bounding, leaving Stefan and me behind in the parking lot. I lean on the hood of the car, arms folded, and watch the children's silhouettes slip and slide out of view, where the ground slopes down to the edge of the briny water. In the stillness I take our bearings. We are poised on the western edge of the Great Basin, where streams and rivers empty into desert lakes like this one—with no outlets, no connection to the sea. No line on my map indicates any hydrologic escape from Mono Lake. In the life cycle of water, this is the geography of terminus.

A topographical map of the Great Basin tells the story of Mono Lake in a series of snaking, soft-gray elevation lines. The roughly two-hundred-thousand-square-mile area is a collection of rock layers that incline toward the center and drain internally. It defies what we commonly hold true—that water falling to Earth finds its way to the oceans through a network of rivers. At Mono Lake it collects as if in a tub and slowly turns salty through evaporation. Three converging blue lines mark the lake's main tributaries—Mill, Lee Vining, and Rush Creeks. These sources come together from the south and the north to create a body of shining azure that reflects the surrounding mountains as though it contains the whole world beneath its surface. But this is only the story of its geography.

The children come running back to the car, chilled, their shoes soaked. They hop around the parking lot trying to convince us they are not cold. They don't want to get back in the car and beg to stay longer. Strictly speaking, our trip to Mono Lake is ill timed: we notice few traces of wildlife, the trail placards are iced over, and there are no ranger tours running. We are the only people here. We make a game of finding shapes in the tufas, the strangely sculpted limestone towers rising stalwart out of the water. Born of centuries of calcium carbonate deposits, they grow up from the lake's sunken springs like jagged insinuating fingers. Just seventy years ago, not even a blink in geologic time, they were barely peeking above the surface of the lake. Today, they stand exposed and scolding because lake levels have fallen dramatically ever since a group of people somewhere else decided they needed the water more than it was needed here.

I clear snow from a placard in the parking lot and learn that Mono Lake is a target in the California Water Wars. Since 1941, the lake's feeder steams have been diverted through an aqueduct to export water three hundred miles away to quench the needs of an expanding Los Angeles. I dig out more maps, trying to visually piece together this history. The brochure from the California Department of Parks and Recreation includes a four-color map with scenic areas marked in green and contrasting tan swaths along the shoreline marking ground privately owned by the City of Los Angeles. A map from the Mono Lake Committee, an organization dedicated to protecting the area's watershed, shows how the aqueduct's siphoning has exposed a ring of lake bed. A dotted line notes where the shoreline should be. But nowhere can I find the path of the aqueduct. None of my maps show where a surveyor might have planted a flag and said, here, here is where we will defy the geography of the ages and set the waters flowing out of the Great Basin.

William Mulholland, a turn-of-the-twentieth-century engineer and director for the Los Angeles Department of Water and Power, masterminded the aqueduct at Mono Lake. It is an impressive series of open channels, tunnels, and pressurized pipes that takes the water on an epic course that skirts

Mountains, carving out the gorge that defines the border between Oregon and Washington. But he doesn't bother detailing Tongue Point, a nearly mile-long peninsula that bespeaks the river's surrender to the sea. Along this outcrop of land, the Columbia's fresh water floats above the denser salt water before soaking into the tides. On the map, where Tongue Point should be, my son has drawn a single, shaky blue arrow that edges off the outline of the continent and points to the words "Pacific Ocean." This uncelebrated marking of the end of the river's twelve-hundred-mile journey troubles me. It suggests that the river is finite, that it has no future. I shift my weight from side to side, lean over his work, and wonder if he can imagine that water travels from land to sea to air, and back. I am uncertain about articulating how, by degrees, one thing becomes another.

The trembling blue arrow reminds me of a fishing trip Stefan and I once took. We bobbed in a rented motorboat in Netarts Bay. I baited crab traps and watched the lapping waters gradually grow up into folding waves until, at some distance, they mixed with the pounding surf. I couldn't fix the point where the marine horizon unequivocally shifted, where I could say, "This is exactly where the bay ends and the sea begins." I was tempted to drop traps farther out to get a better idea of the border between the two, but a sensible fear of the open ocean kept my curiosity in check. I didn't want us to find ourselves caught in rough water in such a small craft, wondering how we got there.

I didn't think about it then, but now know that in cycles of all kinds the transition points are often both elusive and critical. This is the lesson I want my son to learn, that I wish were evident in his drawing. But I can find no good way to suggest that he spend more time drawing Tongue Point other than to say that a shaky blue arrow makes the river's merge with the sea seem inconsequential. I keep quiet because he is working so hard to finish the assignment. Instead, I watch how he goes over and over the line that plots the river's path, the part he moment you say "I do," or are they put in motion, like a chain of reactions, starting from the first time you meet? Some people think it's unusual that my niece is marrying a foreigner, but to me it ripples into the past, to the African American, North American, Polish, and Ukrainian unions of my parents and grandparents. I looked over my shoulder and glimpsed my children, whose eyes scanned the creek banks for any sign of thick haunches and curved antlers. When my daughter squealed, claiming to have spotted a moose, she set our heads turning. It was then that I noticed that the car was still paralleling the creek, moving up current, headed toward the source.

My last trip to Montana, over twenty years ago, was hasty. My boyfriend at the time and I had packed an overstuffed futon into a twenty-year-old Volkswagen Fastback and hurried across the country from San Francisco to New York City. Our only detour was Glacier National Park to drive the Going-to-the-Sun Road during the short seasonal window when the two-lane highway is cleared of snow. In a picture of me taken at the turnout on Logan Pass, the highest point on the road, I straddle the Continental Divide. I am full-face to the camera, my mouth partway open as though in mid-sentence or mid-laugh. We had traded jokes about whether the car would have enough acceleration to power up the climb to 6,646 feet. At the summit we stopped to document the accomplishment. Somewhere behind me in the picture is a signpost that, at the time, I didn't bother to read, but that I now know describes the geographic consequence of the location. The Continental Divide separates the watersheds of the Americas—to the west of it, all rivers drain to the Pacific Ocean; to the east of it, they run to the Atlantic Ocean. Geographers consider it the hydrological apex of North America. But I couldn't tell that standing there. It just looked like other places I'd seen on the trip.

After snapping our photos and taking in the view, we piled back into the car with a new concern for the brakes on the winding descent. We dropped down into the valley and forged across Montana's plains. The mountains appeared fully framed in the rearview mirror, like an improbable movie set, jutting precipitously out of a flat, treeless foreground. At first we raised our eyes every few minutes to watch the reflected image diminish a mile at a time. But finally, we anchored our attention on the road in front of us and plotted our progress on the map, drawing a finger over each town as we rolled east.

When Stefan, the kids, and I arrived on Missoula, we sprang into pre-wedding action, lifting, stacking, folding, and ironing whatever Maya set in our hands. The wedding was small and personal—all of the forty guests were either family or close friends. Maya had planned an elegant outdoor affair that required the help of many hands to succeed on her limited budget. We gathered the morning of to help decorate the tent, polish stemware, tie boutonnières, wrap favors, set tables, transport chairs, and hang flying-insect traps. An hour before the ceremony, everyone scattered to shower and change. When we reunited it didn't seem as though we just had spent the day toiling together in the late summer heat; we admired our handiwork as though strangers had done it. During the processional, my niece walked between her parents and appeared both weak with emotion and driven by anticipation. Curiously, it was my brother I watched most closely. Struck by how much he looked like my father, I couldn't take my eyes off him. All weekend no one had talked about how proud my father would have been to witness his granddaughter's wedding. Maybe no one wanted to feel again the sadness of his death, or maybe no one wanted to admit that we'd learned to celebrate without him.

As my brother passed me in the aisle, I shifted my gaze to my mother, who was perched almost off the edge of her seat in the row in front of me. She had tears in her eyes. I was twelve at my brother's wedding, almost the age of my son, who was fidgeting in the row behind me. My brother's wedding had been far more modest, held in the living room of our Manhattan apartment. We had prepared a vegetarian buffet. I wore my sixth-grade graduation dress. My mother had cried then, too. As my niece reached the altar, I thought that the tears my mother had shed then were the same as the ones she shed now, somehow reconstituted from the memories—good and bad—of other family milestones. Just before the officiant began, a friend leaned over and said, "It won't be long until we see your little one in a long white dress." She meant my seven-year-old daughter, who was the flower girl. It was strange to try to picture my daughter— still a boy-bodied pixie—as a mature woman, and stranger still to imagine her the mother of a child of marrying age. I felt heady and adrift; I wanted to drop anchor, find a mooring. I childishly wished for this moment on Lolo Creek to remain forever present. But the rush of the creek was an unbroken pulse in the background during the exchange of vows and the gifts of rings. At the sake ceremony, Maya and her husband-to-be bowed their heads to take three sips each from three small cups. This is *san san kudo*, which literary translates as "three three nine times," with the number nine symbolizing luck and happiness. Before long, we all headed back to the house to toast the newlyweds, moving slowly through the grass until we were out of earshot of the water that was always on its way and never arriving.

The day after the wedding, Stefan, the kids, and I were the first to leave Missoula, our camping gear packed back into the car for the last stretch of our journey, eleven hours to Oregon. My mother flew west; the rest of the family flew east. After having spent nearly a month on the road, I had lost interest in going anywhere except home. We passed the time in the car singing rounds, playing twenty questions, and arguing. We pressed on uncomfortably to our destination rather than stop too often. Heading south to Kennewick, Washington, we crossed the Columbia River and dropped into Oregon, where we crossed a bend in the river a second time. Back in familiar

⟨⟨   Conversations About Bees

I said: I'm thinking about keeping bees.

He said: That's good, considering everything.

I said: Everything?

We sat in folding chairs on the terrace, my brother and I, one thick Manhattan summer night. The street pulsed like an illuminated artery twelve stories below us. We grew up in this apartment, and he took it over when my parents moved to live near me, on the other side of the continent, in a town that didn't have high-rise buildings, in a place where people considered putting beehives in their backyards.

He said: Yeah, I read the bees are dying.

I said: Well, actually they're disappearing.

He said: Same thing.

I said: Not really.

At my house in Oregon, in every direction the view is of trees—in yards, on hillsides, rising on ranges that divide the valley from the ocean. Drive through my town and here's what you won't see: three-hundred-dollar haircuts, couture, people lined up around the block to get into bars or movies or anywhere. After a decade living in a state where three of the main industries are agriculture, forestry, and fisheries, I had an edge over my brother when talking about nature. I flashed my knowledge like a badge.

I said: It's called colony collapse disorder.

He said: What is?

I said: The disappearing bees.

He said: Oh.

Stefan and I wanted to keep bees because our plum and cherry trees weren't as productive as they used to be. When I left on my trip to New York, the cherry tree branches were weighed down with green stones, baskets-worth of aborted fruit.

I said: When hives fail, the bees leave and never come back.

He said: (Nothing)

I said: It's as if they forget what they're doing or where they belong.

He said: (Nothing)

I said: We don't even know if having bees will help our trees.

He said: Well, it can't hurt.

He was right; it couldn't hurt. That's why Stefan and I were going to give beekeeping a try.

My brother picked up his guitar and folded his body around it like an embrace. He strummed a few notes and let them mix with the rumble of the M20 bus as it lumbered up Eighth Avenue. His silhouette was lit from the lamplight on the other side of the glass terrace door. It was one out of a million lights in our building, on our block, in the neighborhood, on this island of a city. I couldn't make out any stars, so I looked down instead of up. The street seemed far away. I wondered: Do bees even make it up this high?

(

Late in the afternoon, one day in mid-November 2006, a beekeeper in Florida went to check on his hives and discovered that four hundred of them were empty.

He said: I've had die-offs before, but nothing like this.

The bees had gone to forage and had never come back. They'd left their queen behind. A philosopher poet might have stopped to ponder whether the bees had reconsidered their swarm regime to reinvent themselves by scattering into thousands of communities of one. But the beekeeper didn't waste time on such thoughts; he immediately called the agricultural researchers at the state university, looking for answers.

They said: Send in specimens. Send in dead bees from around the hives.

He said: I don't think you get it. There are no dead bees. The bees are gone.

A few months later, the beekeeper's story broke on the news around the country. He became Citizen X of the apiary world, the first one to report a case of colony collapse disorder.

He said: I knew something was wrong before I even opened the first hive.

Millions of bees disappeared without a trace that day. The air was still when the beekeeper got the university researchers on the phone. Even if they had pressed their ears to the receiver, they wouldn't have heard a low-tone death hum in the background; ghost hives are silent. Within the year, other beekeepers made the news—not just in Florida, but also in California, Oklahoma, and Texas. By 2009, cases of colony collapse disorder were reported in thirty-two other states where commercial crops are grown. Voices rose in an alarmed chorus.

They said: One out of every three bites of food we eat depends on pollination by bees.

They said: Food doesn't come from the supermarket.

But what they really meant was that if their bees had problems, then we all had problems.

I first learned about bees in first grade. My teacher gave each student an avocado pit that she'd skewered with toothpicks and suspended in a jar of water.

She said: It will sprout roots and then leaves.

I wanted to say: I don't believe it.

She said: And when it flowers, bees will pollinate it.

I wanted to say: This pit is too big to be a seed.

She said: Wouldn't it be nice to grow avocados at home?

I said: (Nothing)

Bees are the main pollinators of avocados. Maybe my teacher knew that or maybe she didn't. Without bees, avocados would be scarce, and so would blueberries, strawberries, raspberries, or any berries. Kiwis, onions, broccoli, cauliflower, carrots, coffee, cucumbers, apples, almonds, and dozens of other foods would be also hard to come by. I doubt my teacher knew I lived on the twelfth floor of an apartment building. Maybe if she had known, she could have told me how high bees can fly, and maybe she would have had to revise her idea of me growing avocados, if twelve stories up was too high. But it didn't really matter because I was too mistrustful of the experiment to care much about it.

After three weeks, the skewered avocado pits broke open and roots started to emerge from the bottom. In another week or so, stems sprouted out of the tops. I felt ashamed for having doubted my teacher. After all, up until that point in first grade, she had never been wrong about anything, as far as I could tell.

She said: See, it's going to become a tree.

I said: I see.

But I also saw something else. Each morning, when my teacher paced in front of our jars filled with cloudy, yellow water, I thought the rows of avocado plants seemed miserable on the windowsill, where they looked out at the park and saw real plants living real lives. Our classroom must have been like a prison to them, where they were trapped in glass, under constant observation. In two long perfect rows, they looked like an avocado chain gang, serving time and wondering: How did we get ourselves into this mess?

After a few weeks, my teacher replanted the sprouting avocados in plastic pots and let us take them home.

She said: Be careful.

I said: Okay.

She said: Remember to water it.

It's hard to say what happened to my avocado plant. Maybe I left it on the bus or in the elevator. Or maybe I gave it to someone as a present or, more likely, just forgot to take care of it until it died out on the terrace. Of course, it's also possible that my plant ran off in search of other elementary school botanical experiments. Maybe it wanted to start a forest far away from all the jars and toothpicks. Maybe thousands of avocado plants were wandering the streets of New York City after dark, stealthy stalks that had slipped through the hands of the city's schoolchildren, children who were just as happy to imagine them as underground urban orchards, where concrete streets muffled the sound of subterranean bees.

(

Urban beekeeping became legal in New York City in 2010, and within two years there were nearly two hundred registered hives. I had left the city long before that.

The last time I lived in New York City, I rented an apartment with windows that looked into other people's windows. I kept the shades drawn and put a clock in every room because there was no other way to tell the time of day. I bought a ficus tree because I'd read it's healthy to have green, living things where you live. The week after I'd lugged it eight long blocks to my apartment, it was infested with mites. A month later, all the leaves fell off.

I said (to no one): Where did all these bugs come from, anyway?

I like telling people in Oregon that I grew up in New York

City. Those three words—*New, York, City*—provide a ready excuse for bowing out of debates on things like curbside composting and the politics of pesticides. Although I might know a few pros and cons on such subjects, it's not enough to argue a strong point. If people don't make the leap of association from the circumstances of my childhood to my occasional reticence, I give them a little more to go on.

I say: I didn't grow up with a garden.

But what I really mean is that while I might be able to show off to my brother in a short conversation about the plight of the honey bee, I'm a city kid at heart.

It was different for Stefan. He grew up surrounded by orchards and vineyards. When he was a kid, the low-chord buzzing of bees was a springtime soundtrack.

I said: Is that why you became an agricultural scientist?

He said: No.

I said: I bet that's not true.

He said: I don't know what to say to that.

Before we got married, he asked me to edit his dissertation. It was on intercropping systems. I didn't know what that was, so he explained how the food chain depends on plants, and that 80 percent of flowering plants depend on pollination, and that resources are limited, and that we need to find better ways of taking care of people and the land.

I said: Is that what your dissertation is about?

He said: In a way.

Really, his dissertation was a stiff analysis of using woody tree waste as fertilizer, but his passion was to teach people why they should care about how their food is grown.

He said: A lot has to happen before food gets to the table.

While I edited his dissertation, I worked as a grant writer for the Oregon Department of Education in an office building that, as far as I could tell from my cubicle, had no windows. One day, as I raced around trying to finalize a grant proposal, my colleague photocopied and collated the proposal's appendices. As she fed the inch-thick stack of paper into the photocopier, the machine started chewing on the pages. Error lights flashed. The operation came to a halt. She made piles on the floor trying to sort out everything, every few seconds looking up at the clock. We were getting close to our deadline. There was no time to spare. She knew it, and so did our boss.

He said: Jesus. How stupid are you?

She said: (Nothing)

He said: You're going to screw this up for everyone.

She said: (Nothing)

Tears rolled down her face.

I said: Hey, don't talk to her like that.

This got my boss's attention.

I said: If you take a seed, put it in the ground, add water and light, it'll grow.

He stared at me. And because I didn't think he was following my meaning, I spelled it out for him.

I said: And if that plant has flowers and bees, then you have food. Now that's some kind of magic. This is just photocopying.

I think he wanted to apologize or go back in time and take back what he'd said because it looked as though he was replaying the last minute over in his mind. But there was no time for any of that. If we worked together, we could still make the deadline.

He said: Okay.

((

My first garden was in our Oregon house, the house with the pear, cherry, and plum trees. The same year the Florida beekeeper pulled back the curtain on the connection between bees and global food production, Stefan and I were remodeling the house. The first two years, we let the garden go wild while we spent nights and weekends hanging drywall and laying flooring. We'd fling ourselves into plastic lawn chairs after long days spent in dust masks and safety goggles, and we'd look at our overgrown hedges, patchy grass, and neglected rhododendrons. We dreamt about weeding and planting and getting our hands in the dirt. The trees took care of themselves, blooming bright in the spring and bearing fruit in the summer. Stefan and I weren't thinking about the bees then. We had other concerns.

He said: In a couple of days we can close the walls and start mudding the seams.

I said: Can you hold the baby for a second?

He said: And then we can install the floor.

I said: Okay. I can take the baby now.

He said: We'll seal the house just in time for winter.

Maybe the evening news reporting on colony collapse disorder would have caught my attention if the video B-roll had been more compelling. But in the newscasts the bee yards were always empty. The ground wasn't carpeted with apian bodies; the cameramen didn't have to watch where they stepped. The bees were just gone. And without the discomforting sight and sound of dead and dying insects, I didn't feel compelled to put down my drill, hammer, or paintbrush.

It wasn't until years later, when we started having problems with our trees, that I started to pay attention. The experts talked about the effects of climate change, pesticides, and the stresses on bees when they are trucked around the country to pollinate crops. When it came to our trees, I had my own theories. My agriculturally trained husband indulged me.

I said: The problem is the plum tree is too eager for its own good. And the cherry tree is afraid to trust its instincts. The pear tree seems even-keeled.

He said: Is that so?

Stefan spends his days tilling, planting, harvesting, and teaching for a living.

He said: You'd never make it as a farmer.

I said: That's not the point.

He said: The point is that the trees aren't getting pollinated.

The first spring we lived in the house, our yard was an explosion of blossoms. A few weeks after the petals fell, we ate handfuls of cherries while we watched the kids play in the cul de sac and invited neighbors to fill up bowls with fruit. When the summer months heated up, we noshed on plums and spit the pits into the lawn. The pears came on in the fall and were reserved for canning. Whatever was in the high branches went to the birds, the deer ate what fell to the ground, and we took what we wanted and left the rest to rot on the tree. We were spoiled, thinking it would always be so good. But when we started getting less fruit with each passing year, I stopped being so generous with the neighbors; I brought them offerings instead of inviting them over to pick.

One spring, Stefan and I saw hardly any bees in flight. The trees were flush with showy flowers—eager, open, and waiting.

I said: It's like a Greek tragedy out here.

He said: We might not get much fruit this year.

I said: If only it would help to scold the trees or plead with the bees.

He said: Yeah, if only.

((

Pollination is the springtime synchronization of plants and the animals and insects that feed on the nectar and pollen they produce. It happens like a well-timed dance; the partners have to be in seasonal step with one another. In spring, plants shake loose from their winter sleep; they sprout, break buds, and flower. The greening of the landscape is so dramatic you can see it from space. In our corner of Oregon, the spring signal for plants to flower has happened a half day earlier each year, which means the best days for pollination have crept forward on the calendar. Stefan thought the problem with our trees might be that they were getting out of sync with the local bees.

I said: See, the trees are either too eager or insecure.

He said: (Nothing)

I said: Even if we have a hive, won't the bees and trees still be out of step?

He said: Maybe.

I said: And if we have a hive, how can we be sure it won't fail?

He said: We can't.

We had this conversation about bees just before my trip to New York City to visit my brother. We would all come to the same conclusion—it was better to try keeping bees than not.

I said: We'll need to get the gear.

I could picture Stefan in a white smock and veiled hat, a smoker in one hand and hive tool in the other.

I said: Actually, we'll need to get two sets of gear.

This wasn't going to be just his work. I wanted to get in there with the bees too. I wanted to see it all for myself.

I looked into my neighbors' yards and saw their fruit trees and summer vegetables. Our bees would forage not just in our garden, but also in their gardens, and in the gardens of our neighbors' neighbors. Our bees would connect our quarter-acre lot to a collection of lots that was surrounded by a community of farms in a region where local growers were part of a national network of food producers. You would be able to see our bees from the ground, but you would have to soar miles above Earth to begin to trace the complex web tying us all together.

《   Home at the Heart

After twenty years of living as an expatriate in the United States, Stefan announced he wanted to go home. And by *home* he meant the German village where he'd grown up, a hamlet of two hundred households tucked into the northwestern edge of the Black Forest, a slice of southern Germany with undulating valleys and heights. He raised the idea of moving one afternoon while our kids were napping. He had hinted at the idea before, but this time he wanted to discuss it in earnest. We sat in the dining room surrounded by toys and dirty dishes, the morning's detritus frozen in place and waiting for the next round of busy hands. The table was tacky from spilled juice, and there was a small lake of it on the high chair tray. Across the floor was a light sprinkling of Cheerios. They blended in with the hardwood so you didn't notice them at first, but once you looked closely, you realized they were everywhere. I took a seat at the table and cleared away objects on the floor with my foot: a sandal, a Matchbox car, a pacifier. When Stefan said, "I want to move home to Germany," I had been planning for the afternoon, thinking about what I needed to prepare to take the kids to the park.

Now, sitting opposite him, I struggled to shift gears, to focus on a new question: What would I need to move the family to Europe?

Stefan leaned back in his chair, reached around the counter for a sponge, wiped the sticky spot on the table, and cleared a place to rest his hands in front of him. Just a moment before, the clutter had been little more than a reflection of our daily routine, a snapshot of how quickly chaos can penetrate a household with two children still in diapers. I knew I could wrangle things back into shape by dinner, but when I considered the mess through the lens of moving, it took on a heroic scale. Getting us from one day to the next required tidying and stacking, but getting us from one country to another meant sorting, repairing, cleaning, wrapping, and boxing all of the jam-flecked, crayon-marred wood and plastic bits and pieces of our life. Not again, I thought. Or at least, not again so soon. We had only recently moved into the new house in the new town to be closer to the new tenure-track teaching position Stefan had landed. And before this house and this job, there had been others; we'd relocated four times in three years, each time spanning the continent, from the West Coast to the East Coast and back, packing and repacking our lives in cardboard U-Haul boxes. Before we finally settled in Oregon, we had landed here, in New Hampshire. This location had a tribal logic that made us think we could put down roots—we were only a few hours from my family in New York City and were closer to Stefan's family than we had ever been before (although it still involved a trans-Atlantic flight). The thought of pulling up stakes again, just as we'd broken down and recycled the last box from our last move, stunned me. When I asked Stefan if he wanted to go back home because he was homesick, he said the feeling was more diffuse than that, more like an imbalance in the air, in his blood, or in his memories.

"It's not *Heimweh*. It's *Heimat*," he said. "If you know what I mean."

But I didn't know.

The German word for "homesickness," *Heimweh*, translates literally from *Heim*, meaning "home," and *Weh*, meaning "woe." The compound word is from Swiss dialect and originally referred to a longing for the mountains. According to its etymology, *Heimweh* was first introduced into the German language in the seventeenth century by Swiss mercenaries who pined for the sight of the Alps as they battled their way across central Europe fighting for foreign armies with their signature pikes. The English use of the word, according to the American Psychological Association, is neither about home nor sickness in the way we typically think about a sense of place or a disease. Instead, its definition describes distress caused by an actual or anticipated separation from the people, objects, locales, and customs that make us feel loved, protected, and secure. Homesickness can flare at any age and is as likely to afflict a forty-year-old on a business trip as an eight-year-old at summer camp. We learn to stave off its effects by re-creating familiar patterns. We eat foods that remind us of home; we seek out people who either know something about where we are from or are willing to listen to us describe it; we keep track of our surroundings, noting how similar or dissimilar they are from what we miss.

In the two decades since he'd arrived in the United States, Stefan had married and started a family. He sang the kids songs he'd grown up with and read them his favorite stories. At least once a week we ate dark bread, boiled potatoes, herring, radishes, and hard cheese for dinner, a typical evening meal where he's from. In winter he cross-country skied whenever he could and came home windburned and elated from his time in the woods, which were not quite like the woods he knew in Germany but were close enough to stir his memories. Sitting across from him now at the dining table, I watched him absentmindedly poke the beads of water left behind from where he'd wiped with the sponge. He seemed a lifetime away, or maybe he was just searching for the best words to tell me why he thought we should leave.

Like the word *Heimweh*, *Heimat* has a sense of home at its heart, but there is no direct translation to English. For the student of German looking for a quick definition, *Heimat* means "home" or "home country." But search beyond a pocket edition of a Langenscheidt dictionary and the meaning quickly grows complex. Peter Blickle writes in his book on the critical theory of the German idea of homeland that some translations of *Heimat* relate it to national identity (such as fatherland and nation), whereas others emphasize a person's individual and emotional ties to their origins (as in birthplace or homestead). The word connotes a relationship to the earth (as in native soil and habitat). Germans use *Heimat* as a substitute for the word "Germany," Austrians use it to mean "Austria," and the Swiss to mean "Switzerland." Even more curiously, and perhaps the greatest testament to its intangibility, *Heimat* is sometimes translated as "paradise." Put aside any ambition to pinpoint a single, concrete meaning, and you open up a broader discussion of *Heimat* in the linguistic and psychosocial traditions of the Germanic people. Stripping the word bare of its connotations of region, landscape, environment, and purity, Nietzsche called it the mythical womb of the mother, and Freud referred to it as a key to unlock the feminine and sexual underpinnings of the uncanny. With no context for the word in English, the interpretations are dizzying.

"So, what is *Heimat*, then?" I said.

"*Heimat* is *Heimat*," Stefan said. "It's home, but not a place."

"Is it where you grew up?"

"It's everything about where I grew up but nothing in particular."

I felt as if he were reciting riddles.

"Then," I said, with more condescension than I intended, "what's the point in going?"

The longer we circled the definition, the clearer it became that he knew, and had always known, something that I might never understand. Blickle writes that all native German speakers think they know what *Heimat* is, but as soon as you ask them to explain it, they struggle. Had I known that from the start, I might have skipped the semantics lesson and spent the sacred quiet that is naptime thinking about a more relevant question: Could I leave the United States for good?

❨

One of Stefan's favorite stories is how he came to the United States. When he tells it, he begins with a confession of academic failure. After he barely passed his high school exit exams, Stefan's parents supported his decision to do an apprenticeship while he figured out whether he wanted to go to college. He hired on with a strawberry farm and learned the business from the ground up. He fell in love with the land. After the apprenticeship, he decided to go to college to study agricultural science and returned each summer to the strawberry farm to till and plant, tend and harvest. The shortest version of his emigration tale chronicles his apprenticeship, university studies, and an opportunity to study abroad. But Stefan rarely follows this straight tack and instead almost always detours to tell how, in early 1990, the year he left Germany, he worked one last summer on the strawberry farm alongside a crew of Serbian and Bosnian migrant pickers. At the time, tensions were rising as Muslim Bosnians and Orthodox Christian Serbs positioned for independence following the breakup of Yugoslavia. Within two years, the region would erupt into a bloody war. The atmosphere on the farm that season was bewildering. One moment the Bosnians and Serbs reminisced about the homeland they loved and shared, and the next moment, in voices edged with anger and anticipation, they described how they might be killing each other in the streets within a few months' time.

There was nothing magical about the work on the strawberry farm; it was hard labor from morning to dark. But for those few months, the workers moved shoulder to shoulder in the rows, fingers stained red from the picking. In the fields of someone else's farm, on the land in someone else's country, the tinder of politics never ignited as the workers toiled toward a common purpose: to pick enough strawberries—tens of thousands of them—to earn enough money to send home and create new opportunities. It is easy to miss the reflective leap in Stefan's story, the tenuous bridge between this last summer on the farm and his decision to leave Europe. He never says that he was searching, like the Bosnian and Serbian workers, for new possibilities in a new land. He never says that the workers reflected his ambivalence about leaving the ground he knew best. He never says they demonstrated how soberly such a decision should be made. And yet he almost always mentions them whenever he talks about the time he left home. Over the years, I have watched Stefan walk the rows of his research fields in the United States, bend down to pick up a clod of earth, and roll it in his hand until it falls through his fingers. It's as though this sifting is a search for something elemental in the earth beneath his feet, something he can't quite grasp.

After the apprenticeship and three years of university in Germany, Stefan applied for an exchange program in the United States. It was a chance to pursue a passion for sustainable farming and the practices he thought were essential to feeding the world. When his American professor offered to extend his sponsorship, Stefan stayed for two years to complete his master's degree. And when the same professor suggested he remain to do his doctorate, Stefan stayed longer still. He always thought he would eventually go back to Germany, but when he met and married me shortly before his doctoral defense, those plans were shelved. "I came for nine months and never left," he says as the punch line to his coming-to-America story. During the three years it took to finalize his permanent residency status, we moved four times and had two children. Stefan's parents never imagined that his path to an agricultural apprenticeship would end in his pursuit of advanced degrees in an adopted land. So to make up for the separation, we committed to spending our summers with them in Europe. His parents helped us buy plane tickets, and we sought teaching and consulting jobs with nine-month appointments. Every time we moved somewhere new, we considered proximity to airports and gradually mastered the art of long-distance air travel with infants.

Each summer, emerging into the concourse of Frankfurt Airport, Stefan was a man transformed. He didn't change in bold strokes; the shift was more understated. He didn't have the clean-shaven face, smart glasses, or red jeans that German fashion always seems to demand. But even with his five o'clock shadow, low-slung chinos, and faded T-shirts, he always fit in. It was not so much about how he looked but how he carried himself, how his body moved in the landscape like a creature in its natural habitat. I think because of our everyday intimacies— because I knew the rise and fall of his breath at night, the scent of his skin when he held me in his arms—I noticed something unfamiliar about him each time we arrived in Germany. In Germany the small of his back had a more delicate tilt, which translated up his spine and made his chest and head ease forward. The end effect was a faint alteration in his expression—a change so quiet that others easily missed it, and yet it made him look to me like a completely different person. This realignment was most noticeable when he spoke to friends and family in Badisch, his regional dialect. Badisch was the language of his boyhood adventures in the woods behind his father's house; it was the language whispered before his first real kiss with the girl whose name he later forgot; it was the language of his hotheaded arguments with his brother and the loving coos from his grandmother. When Stefan speaks Badisch his voice is deeper, his shoulders drop, and he smiles more in conversation, even when he is not the one talking. I have often wondered: If language can change the shell of a body, can it also change the nature of a person's personality? When I asked Stefan whether he thought that he not only *sounds* different but also *is* different when speaking in dialect, he shrugged and said, "How should I know?"

When I first met Stefan, he still made small mistakes when speaking English, saying things like "You better don't" instead of "You better not." But such slips were rare, emerging mostly when he was in a hurry. In our day-to-day lives, negotiating the price of the cars we bought and then resold when we moved, discussing the details of apartment lease agreements, or wrangling with utility companies to open and close accounts, he sounded American. Subtle hints reminded me that English was not his first language, but I never thought there was a better way for him to say what he meant. That is, until the first time we traveled to Germany, and he slipped into dialect and used words and phrases that made sense only in his region, to his people. The German philosopher Martin Heidegger wrote that the essence of language is rooted in dialect, and that through dialect speaks the region and, therefore, the ground beneath our feet. The body and the mouth, in the sounding of words, belong to the earth and its growth, and from that growth we derive a sense of indigenousness—a sense of *Heimat*. The combination of voice and ground conjures an image of Stefan on the strawberry farm, filching berries from the picking baskets, berries still warm from the sun and coated with a silt so fine it is undetectable to the palette. I imagine that that combination of sweetness and grit must have tasted like his childhood, and the childhood of his father, and of his father's father.

((

Nap time was just long enough to start a list of pros and cons of moving to Germany. This was always our first step. Before we had a chance to get attached to a particular opinion about whether to stay or go, we tried to pull together an unbiased list of considerations. We were familiar with these lists with so many relocations under our belts. Stefan got up from the dining table to get a pad and pen. I anticipated the first questions: What kind of job could he find? What about my consulting work? How much money would we need for the first few months? Would we take a financial hit selling the house? Could we find a place to live near Stefan's parents? Did we want to? This list would be the first of many, rewritten and reconsidered over several weeks as we inventoried our various issues and concerns. Then we would make a matrix to further dissect our options. The matrix would keep the decision-making process objective—or at least give it that appearance. Whether we agreed or disagreed about what we wanted to do, we liked to think that the matrix would prevent us from making choices based solely on emotion. Although it didn't strip away our prejudices, it at least helped us see where they were strongest.

But before considering our future, I took stock of my present. I had two children under four, a house I could hardly keep up, and a consulting business that landed contracts in the nick of time to help pay the bills. I could barely predict the outcome of any single day but had assumed that whatever happened would happen in the United States. In truth, I didn't want to make another list or another matrix, because it seemed that we had attained our goal of buying a house and settling down. Now, just as our lives were coming into focus, the idea of moving to Germany had skewed the perspective. It was as if I was looking through the wrong end of a pair of binoculars—I could still see the same content of my life, but what had been near was now far away.

Stefan returned with pad and pen.

"Where should we start?" he said.

Where indeed?

I leaned my forehead into my hands and spotted a scrap of paper under the couch. I crawled to collect it. In recent weeks our nine-month-old had started eating paper. She scuttled across the floor whenever our backs were turned, shoving envelopes, receipts, and gum wrappers into her mouth. The pediatrician suspected a pica—a craving to eat inedible objects—that was triggered by an iron deficiency. We started her on an iron supplement and kept mail, documents, and newspapers out of reach. I snatched the paper from under the couch and pressed it into my pocket, but instead of getting up, I stayed on the floor to appreciate the room from a baby's vantage point. Would our daughter even miss this house? Would one place look like another through her infant eyes? At what age do you start to develop a sense of home? Only this was clear to me: we couldn't move before the pica was resolved. It would be impossible to keep loose paper off the floor while I packed. Before I had the kitchen dishes boxed, her belly would be tied up with wads of cellulose. I stood up and joined Stefan, who was already jotting down notes. I decided to put faith in our system: first the lists, then the matrix. After all, no one was suggesting we start packing as soon as the kids woke up. And yet, unlike the many other relocation decisions we had weighed and balanced, I sensed that something unique was at play. It had to do with ephemeral smells, elusive dreams, and muscle memories. It had to do with an ancestral call to reclaim what was at once familiar and intangible. It had something to do with our future as a family and everything to do with Stefan's past. How do you catalog that as pros and cons?

Over the course of the next few weeks, we started gathering information. Stefan reconnected with friends and old colleagues in Germany to explore potential job options. He called realtors to check out the rental market. I reviewed my client list to see what, if any, work I might be able to do overseas. I scanned real estate websites to gauge how fast houses in our area were selling and called our accountant to find out what our tax liability would be if we put the house on the market. I thought about what I would do all day in Germany if I couldn't work and toyed with the appeal of being a stay-at-home *Hausfrau*. But I spent most of my time thinking about what I would miss. I picked things up—ceramic bowls and vases, framed photos, coffee table books—and wondered: What would make the cut when it came time to pack? One afternoon I pondered the lamp that I'd had since second grade, the one that no longer worked. Would I miss it? And what about the glider rocker I'd used to nurse the kids or the antique highboy I bought with my mother for my fourteenth birthday? Surely we'd leave behind our collection of *National Geographic* magazines. It was one thing to cart them back and forth across the country, but quite another to ship them overseas. For weeks I was fixated on things—how much they weighed, whether they were breakable, if I could fit them in my pocket. One afternoon I remembered a conversation I'd had with Stefan during one of our summer visits to Germany. We were sitting at an outdoor café, when he said, "I miss this."

"What?" I said, darting my eyes around, trying to guess where he'd fixed his gaze.

I could have pointed out countless things: the waitress in a dirndl, the apple cake on the table, or the backdrop of rolling hills of *Zwetschgen* trees weighted down with plums. Or was it the scent of cut wood and manure mingled with the aroma of sugar and steamed milk? It was *Kaffee* and *Kuchen* time—the afternoon hour for coffee and cake in a café not far from a dairy.

What did he miss?

"I don't know," he said. "Just all of this."

"This," I learned over time, was not something that I could pack in our bags and bring back to the United States. "This" was not something I could memorize, purchase, or fabricate. From the first year of our relationship, I had looked for such tangibles, anticipating that one day Stefan might want to return home. I thought that if I could make our home in the United States feel more like his in Germany, he might be satisfied to live the rest of his life abroad. But the things that he missed were not for the taking; they entered through the pores of his skin, filtered through his lungs, and wetted his eyes. What he missed was beyond my grasp; it wasn't anything I could put on the mantel or hang in the kitchen. It wasn't anything that needed bubble wrap and a box marked "fragile." Stefan carried his sense of *Heimat* with him.

In 1984, German director Edgar Reitz produced a made-for-TV movie called *Heimat*. The fifteen-hour, eleven-episode production captivated the attention of 25 million West Germans, over half of the country's population. Reitz produced the series to unite a nation that was still looking to understand itself in the generation that inherited the shame of the Second World War. No doubt, five years later, with the fall of the Berlin Wall, this same generation was scratching its collective head, once again trying to figure out its place in history. It is difficult to imagine what single portrait of the United States—past or present—would appeal to over 160 million Americans. Set your mind wandering across almost four million square miles of mountain ranges, deserts, plains, forests, and wetlands and try to describe the signature geographical feature; move back and forth through the cultural divide of north and south, east and west, and taste every region's unique flair for barbeque sauce; read every story of immigration, slavery, genocide, up-by-the-boot-strap triumph and loss, and imagine how many stories have gone untold; ask a million people what the United States of America means to them and get as many answers. When I travel abroad and people ask me where I am from, I tell them New York City, which inevitably prompts them to say, "Oh, you're American." Yes, I nod, although I consider these two concepts different. As a New Yorker, I know how yellow mustard on a hot salted pretzel makes my lips tingle; I know the acrid smell of urine in the subway station on a summer evening; I know how, in a snowstorm, taxis sound as if they are driving on compressed cotton. Such things might be familiar and in-grained in a New Yorker, but they hardly scratch the surface of what it means to be American. And while I couldn't pinpoint what it means to be from here, I knew I didn't want to leave.

A few months after he first raised the idea of moving, Stefan was invited to interview for a job he'd applied for that was near where he'd grown up. He didn't have much time to prepare. He bought a plane ticket and a new suit, found substitutes for his classes, and researched the company. The day before he left, we talked about what it might mean if he got the job. In all the time we'd thought about the move, we'd reached an impasse, feeling that it would be impossible to make a decision until the moment one had to be made.

"If I get an offer, they might need me to tell them quickly," he said.

"I know," I said.

From the time Stefan first suggested we move, my focus had been more on whether I could see myself living in Germany than whether I could imagine myself leaving the United States. He knew how to be away from home; he had spent more than two decades adapting to life here. I worried that I was in for a rude surprise because I had had no equivalent training. But each time that anxiety rose up in my throat, I swallowed it back down, thinking about the months we visited every year, the friends I'd made there, and my fluency in German. Surely those things would smooth the transition. But something else ate at me, an uncertainty that didn't come so easily to the surface and seemed to squat in my belly.

Some years before, on a trip to visit his family, Stefan's father asked us to help him figure out how, after he'd died and been cremated, we could get our hands on his ashes. In those days in Germany it was illegal to release cremated remains to family members because it was not permitted to scatter ashes on public or private land; they had to be interred. One evening around the dinner table, we plotted an outrageous caper for smuggling my father-in-law's body into France, where the rules for cremation are more relaxed. In France, his remains would be returned to us, and then we could smuggle the ashes back into Germany and release them in the Black Forest, where he had played as a boy and later watched his boys play as children. The conversation had been amusing at the time, but it came into sharp focus now as Stefan packed for his trip.

"Can you imagine yourself living in Germany?" he asked me as he folded shirts to put in his bag.

"I can see myself living there," I said after a while. "I just can't see myself dying there."

Stefan stopped what he was doing. "Yeah, I know what you mean."

And for the first time in our discussion about moving, it seemed we finally were speaking the same language.

❰ Forgotten Winters

Shortly after the November 2012 Palestinian rocket attacks, I received a series of misdialed long-distance calls from Israel. I'd received these calls before, but never so many in one day. This time, like the other times, I didn't recognize the voices on the other end of the line. I could only make out the two names the callers repeated as single-word questions:

"Michael?"

"Michelle?"

I paused. They didn't speak English, and I didn't speak Hebrew.

"They live next door now," I said slowly.

There was silence on the other end, and then the line went dead.

Whenever I got these calls, I never hung up first. I waited in case someone came to the receiver to leave a message in a language I could understand. But even though it seemed that any translation was unlikely, I kept the handset pressed to my ear. Sometimes there were whispers in the background; other times I just heard breathing. I had the luxury of holding on because my world wasn't exploding around me; there was no threat of a missile coming through my kitchen window. So, I waited for them to end the call because it seemed the least I could do.

Most of Michael and Michelle's close friends and family knew that they now lived next door and had their new phone number. But these weren't the people calling my house. I was getting calls from the second and third tier of relations in Michael and Michelle's lives—distant cousins and acquaintances—people, I thought, who still had the old number jotted down on a slip of paper, half-hidden behind drawings affixed to the refrigerator. In a crisis, it is comforting to hear your own voice in concert with others, to remind yourself and anyone who will listen that you are still alive. That's what those slips of paper on the refrigerator are for.

Two years before the rocket attacks, Michael and Michelle had moved from a settlement in southern Israel to our Oregon college town. Michael's company had transferred him, and Michelle gave up her teaching job to become an ex-pat, stay-at-home mom. During their first year, they rented our house and gave our phone number to loved ones back home. Stefan and I rented them our house because we were planning on spending a sabbatical year in Germany with our kids. When Michael and Michelle first arrived, they weren't sure how long they wanted to stay in the United States but thought a year was ample time to decide whether to return to Israel, stay in the United States, or move somewhere else. But it turned out that a year wasn't quite enough time to reach that decision; they were just settling into our place as we were starting to pack to come home. "Can you extend your sabbatical?" Michael joked in an email. "No," we wrote back, avoiding any confusion about the fact that we knew where home was and were eager to reclaim it. When we returned, Michael and Michelle had wandered only as far as a rental house across the street. They figured they would give themselves another year before committing to anything permanent.

We first met Michael and Michelle during their week-long scouting trip. A relocation specialist from Michael's company drove them from appointment to appointment to arrange everything from school registrations for their children to filing residency paperwork. In some ways, Stefan and I were going through similar stages of frenzy as we prepared to leave the United States, but there was an elemental difference in the transitions our two families were about to make: while we knew we were coming back to Oregon in twelve months, Michael and Michelle couldn't see that far into their future. Consequently, it surprised me when they told us that despite the uncertainty of their long-term plans, they had already sold their house in Israel. Michael showed us pictures of the custom, stone home they had built from the ground up, pointing out the hand-painted tiles Michelle had designed to adorn the bathrooms, kitchen, and entryway. He spoke of the house like you would of a child who had unexpectedly passed away—with tenderness and the fruitless hope that it would return one day. When I asked why they hadn't rented their house, Michelle said in broken phrases, "When another cleans, then it is not like before." Michael elaborated, saying that they didn't think they would find anyone to care for the house the way they had, so they had decided to let it go rather than fret about what condition they would find it in later. Michelle drew her lips in. If at first this decision seemed foolish to me, I understood it better in the context of how picky Stefan and I were being about finding the "perfect" renters. In our case, a year was long enough for strangers to feel comfortable in our space—to set out their pictures and put glasses where I usually stacked dishes—but not long enough for them to feel completely at home. But Michael and Michelle were facing an unknown number of years away, after which it might be difficult to buff out the dents left behind by other people's furniture and eliminate the faint hints of perfume and sweat saturating the grout of the tile floors.

"The sale is done," Michael said, closing the viewer on his phone. "So, that's that."

Stefan and I gave Michael and Michelle a room-by-room tour of our house. Michelle quietly tested the minor mechanics of things—the spray function on the kitchen faucet and the dimmer switches in the livingroom. Michael was more vocal, projecting out loud what their lives would be like in each room, first telling Michelle in Hebrew and then translating into English. My office would become his office. Stefan's office would be a playroom. "There's lots of space for dishes," Michael said inspecting the kitchen. "That's good because we keep kosher." At first it made my jaw set listening to him occupy our home in his imagination, but later Stefan reminded me that Michael and Michelle had asked the kinds of questions—Are there instructions for the lawnmower? What kind of products should be used to clean the tub?—that signalled they intended to take good care of the house.

The day of the November rocket attack, I walked across the cul-de-sac to tell Michelle that her friends had been trying to reach her. I'd delivered similar news before, like the times there had been a border breach and a bus bombing. Those two events hadn't directly affected Michael and Michelle's old town, and I'd only received two or three overseas calls on those days. But today was different, and based on the volume of misdialings, I worried that things might be more serious. Michelle saw me from the kitchen window and waved me to come in. I heard her on the phone as I shut the front door and took a seat at the little table by the window and watched her rinse dishes while talking into a headset. She turned to me and mouthed, "My mother."

I sometimes wandered over to Michelle's when we were both home with our kids in the limbo of late afternoon, when it's too late to go anywhere and too early to start dinner. Her English had improved in the two years since she'd arrived, and we would sit, talk, and drink tea while children floated in and out or crowded in front of the TV. We joked about her schemes to find a wife for the cul-de-sac's only bachelor, and she detailed the bargains she'd landed on Craigslist. She showed me her latest ceramics projects and I tried to convince her to try snowboarding. She'd shake her head and say, "My people are from the desert." She gave me her mother's recipe for Moroccan tea biscuits and we discussed how to adjust the ingredients to accommodate my daughter's food allergies. We talked about the minutiae that can feel so important in the background of an uneventful day and never broached two topics: religion and politics. I can't say why she never brought them up, but I know I avoided them because I was embarrassed by how little I knew about the Middle East. I paid attention when there were headlines but then lost the thread of the debate after a few days. From our quiet cul de sac, the Israeli-Palestinian conflict was something I could tune out by using geography as a balm to dull my conscience. It was all so far away. But on the days when strangers telephoned and their voices cracked—*Michael? Michelle?*—a naïve question nagged me: Why was peace so difficult? With no real understanding of that region's centuries-long tangle of religion, politics, and culture, I could think of it only this way: people will fight forever if they feel their home is threatened.

"They are all calling," Michelle, said after hanging up the phone. "A rocket hit the house next to my brother-in-law's." I told her they were calling my phone too.

I doubted Michelle worried about missiles exploding in our cul de sac. I doubted she regularly watched the skies in apprehension or tuned her ears for the cry of air-raid sirens. And if she silently blessed her children each time they left the house, I guessed it was more from habit than any deep-seated fear that she may never see them again.

"Everyone is alright," she said.

This time, I thought. "That's a relief," I said.

Michelle pulled two teacups from the cupboard and told me

some of the details her mother had shared. The house that was hit was badly damaged, but not unsalvageable. The attack had come as a surprise, but everyone had had enough time to get to the shelters. She poured the tea. I watched to see if her hands were shaky, but she had a steady hold on the teapot.

"These things happen," she said.

I thought, not here, they don't.

And with that thought I recognized the flare of judgment that living in the United States was better than living in Israel because it seemed safer. But who was I kidding? America was not only the site of one of the most horrific terrorist attacks in history but also has one of the highest homicide rates of any developed nation. Still, the fact that no one was in the next town firing armaments at us counted for something. Halfway through the first cup of tea we turned to other subjects—dinner plans and weekend chores—and gradually the voices from the misdialed calls faded in my mind, muffled by the comforting talk of the mundane.

A few months after the rocket attacks, Michael and Michelle invited Stefan, the kids, and me over for cake and coffee. Our children and their two wolfed down their slices and then disappeared. Their voices piped up in the background from all corners of the house like a mistuned chorus. As we settled on sofas and chairs, Michael and Michelle told us that they planned to move back to Israel in the spring. When we asked them why, they came at their answer from odd angles.

"Well, we are here almost three years, and I still don't understand this town's obsession with football," Michael said.

I thought I had misheard him or that he had misspoken, but he stayed with the topic.

"Every Monday, everyone is asking, 'Did you see the game? What did you think about the game?'"

It was true, our town is home to a PAC-12 university with a dedicated, tailgating fan base that suffers through mostly losing seasons. But I didn't see the connection between the fall football schedule and Michael and Michelle's decision to move.

"Football is not me," he said. "And it will never be me."

A few times a year, Michael traveled to Israel for work and each time he returned he slipped into a depression brought on by longing. For the first weeks after he got back, he talked about everything he missed—the heat, the sea, the olives, the fig trees—and complained about football, regardless of the season. So his current gripe did not seem completely unusual, even if it seemed signifcantly more urgent.

Michael set his plate down and leaned forward with his hands over his knees as if the coffee table were a campfire. He told us the story of how he and Michelle first met. Their first date included an adventurous ride on an ATV. The conditions were bad that night and the machine had gotten bogged down in a muddy field. Michelle had to get off, wearing new slacks and her best shoes, to help push the ATV out of the muck.

"I wanted to make a good impression because I'd built the ATV myself," he said.

Michael told us that it had taken years to salvage parts and save money for tools to build the machine. He spent his spare hours with his brothers and friends dreaming of ways to make it run faster, smoother, and stronger.

"It wasn't like here," he said, referring to our bachelor neighbor who had spent the last year building a Baja rally car and ordering parts whenever he needed them. "We had to make parts."

Michelle passed around a platter of grapes. She had tears in her eyes.

"And I think about the children," she said. She wondered out loud what would happen if they stayed in the United States without being surrounded by aunts, uncles, cousins, and grandparents.

"Who will hold their faces in their hands and kiss them?"

she said. She cradled her own face, as if she had forgotten that same feeling.

It was difficult to know what to say, particularly because it was as if Michael and Michelle were voicing their reasons for leaving for the first time and couldn't believe their own ears. What may have been intended as a crisp explanation melted into a messy expression of intangibles. How do you put home into words?

"There are so many beautiful places," Michelle said, closing her eyes and recreating the healing salinity of the Dead Sea, the oases of the Judean dessert, the archaeological remains at Masada. It reminded me of something Pablo Neruda had written: that when we are far away from our country, we forget its winters and instead remember only green landscapes, bright flowers, and "the blue sky of the national anthem."

"We hope you will come see us," she said, sounding as if part of her had already crossed the Atlantic and was now waiting for the rest of her to arrive on the shores of the Mediterranean Sea.

This wasn't the first time Michael and Michelle had invited us to visit them in Israel. I replied as I usually did, saying, "Yes, we'll come sometime." I had always been open to the possibility of visiting them there when the idea of traveling to a war zone only had been theoretical. But now, in the context of their imminent departure, the invitation wielded more weight.

"How far will you be from the Gaza Strip?" Stefan said.

"The new house will be like our old one," Michael said. "Maybe twenty miles from the border."

I thought about what I'd miss when they moved. I liked when they wandered by with their kids to eat cherries off our tree or when they brought us bowls of tomatoes from their garden. They joined us for Thanksgiving and had us over for Seder. Lego figures, princess tiaras, sidewalk chalk, and Nerf rockets from both houses often got mixed up in various plastic tubs of toys that we kept in our garages. We carted each other's kids to the swimming pool and enjoyed impromptu picnics on the front lawn, and yet we weren't close enough to talk about the hard things like whether listening to college football fans drone on about the weekend game was a small price to pay for keeping their children out of harm's way.

In July 2014, only a few months after Michael and Michelle had emptied their house and set out for the airport, Israel launched Operation Protective Edge, a military action in the Hamas-governed Gaza Strip. The Israeli bombardment was followed by Palestinian rocket attacks. Had Michael and Michelle still been in the United States, my phone would have been ringing off the hook. But now, I was the one wishing I had a phone number taped to the refrigerator. Without a way to call them or their family, I emailed Michael to see if he, Michelle, and the kids were safe. After a few days, Michael wrote back that they could hear the explosions well and hoped that because their town was so small that the Palestinians would not bother to "waste" a missile on them. Michelle had left the house with the kids to stay with family in a town farther from the border; he had stayed behind because he needed to keep working. He didn't comment on the country's politics, instead shifting to family news: the kids were back to school, and Michelle was back to work. Life was back to normal.

"I know it's not the right timing," he wrote. "But still we'd love you all to come next summer." They had a guesthouse ready.

When I read that, I thought: home is wherever you are tethered, and there can be any number of things—a person, place, or memory, a scent, sound, or texture—on the other end of the line between you and where you feel you belong. It seemed that even with the bombing, Michael and Michelle were glad of their decision to move back to Israel. My only frame of reference for understanding their choice was when, immediately following the September 11 attack in New York City, I decided the best thing to do was to drive from our house in New Hampshire to my parent's apartment in Manhattan. I was in a supermarket parking lot when I heard the news that the North Tower had been struck. I was listening to the radio with my son in the back seat. My first impulse was to take him and head to New York.

I drove back to our house and started collecting what I needed for the trip and, a few moments later, Stefan pulled into the driveway. He ran up the walkway and stormed in the door.

"You can't go home," he said. He'd heard the news on the way to work and turned the car around, anticipating I might be planning to leave.

He convinced me to wait until I could reach my family and when, hours later, I finally did, they convinced me to stay where I was. They said it was no place for the baby. It was crazy on the roads. It was impossible to know what might happen next. But only one argument persuaded me to stay put.

"If we have to evacuate the city," my brother said, "we might have to prove we have a place to go out of state."

In the days that followed the razing of the World Trade Center, I thought about other New York City Septembers when we had shopped at Macy's for school shoes and walked back to the apartment swinging red and white bags. On the way home, we'd stop at the Italian bakery for cherry ices and lick the sticky liquid off our hands. In the weeks and months after the terrorist attack, I held fast to those memories—layers of simple joys that stretched like gauzy dressings around a weeping wound. Michael and Michelle had talked to us about the sea, desert oases, and ancient ruins that make Israel special. But when they boarded their plane, holding their children's hands, I think they were more likely enticed by the promise of the powder-green olives, lightly coated with dust from the wind and dangling in clusters from gnarled limbs, ripe for the taking. With just sixteen hours of flying time, those olives must have been so close they could almost taste them.

⟨ Episodes in People Watching

Standing at the counter at the public swimming pool, I waited to buy a family punch pass and watched my son watch the man watching my daughter. The kids were ten feet behind me, playing in the tile foyer by the front doors. Meilo rocketed his Transformer through the air while Dahlia tried to pick a penny off the floor. At almost two years old, Dahlia had the toddling charm that comes with chubby legs and a shifting center of gravity; it always seemed she might tip over at any moment. She hopped her sandaled feet on either side of the penny, lowered her diapered bottom into a squat, and tried to pry the coin from the floor. When she only managed to slide it around, it prompted her to do another round of hopping, accented with bursts of giggling. Her hair hung in a veil around her face, so even if she'd looked up, it was unlikely that she would have noticed the man watching her. But I saw him. And I saw my son see him.

The man appeared to be in his early eighties and moved with the stiff intention of someone who had been warned more than once about the risks of breaking a hip. He approached Dahlia and stood within a few feet of her, smiling while she hopped and squealed. I took mental notes: he didn't kneel down, reach out a hand, talk to her, or try to draw her attention. But he towered at almost six feet tall, which made her look like she might fit in his pocket. I triangulated the distances between the man, Dahlia, and me and felt confident that he'd never get her out of my sight before I could tackle him. When I handed the pool receptionist my debit card to pay for the punch pass, I kept my body facing the children.

Meilo stopped playing and stared at the man in the un-selfconscious way children do when they think no one can see them. He called his sister's name in a loud whisper and sounded like a reluctant movie hero trying to warn the innocent without revealing his hiding place. At five years old, Meilo was the big kid of the house and was often frustrated by his baby-sister-turned-toddler because she never did what he said. This time, instead of ignoring her when she didn't answer, he took action. He pushed his Transformer into his pocket, crossed the few feet to where Dahlia was, reached down and took her by the shoulder, and told her to stand up. Maybe she sensed that something important was happening or maybe she'd lost interest in the penny, because she didn't fuss when she got to her feet. Meilo wrapped his arms around her, crossing his hands in front of her chest. He didn't take his eyes off the man. Without speaking any words his message was clear: "She's with me." In the few moments that Dahlia consented to stand still in her brother's embrace, the spell was broken; the man walked over to a woman, who looked about his age, and the couple left the building together. Only then did Meilo unclasp his grasp and let Dahlia return to her work on the floor. Before reaching for his Transformer and going back to his game, Meilo shot me a bitter look that seemed to say, "Where were you in all this?" I smiled. I wanted to tell him what a good job he'd done, how proud I was, how important it is to trust your instincts. But I figured there would be time for that later—after swimming, after dinner and bath time, after the edge of the day had softened.

((

Stefan and I had decided to raise our kids in a small town, the kind of place where we'd run into friends at the farmer's market. So we carved out a life in a community that was similar in pace to the small German village where he'd grown up and that was the opposite of the taut urgency of New York City. We had things here that I'd never had growing up as a kid—things like neighbors who appeared unannounced in the garage to borrow ladders, a postal carrier who exchanged pie recipes while standing in front of the mailboxes in the cul de sac, and strangers who greeted each other on the bus. For me, moving to a small town meant learning a new set of survival skills, ones that were more about cordiality and openness and less about mistrust and boundaries. Here, I didn't need to put on my "New York face," a virtual mask that told people to get out of my way or else. Instead, I waved courteously at drivers who stopped at pedestrian crosswalks and made eye contact with coffee-shop waitresses. I waited patiently when people unloaded a full shopping cart of groceries in the line reserved for twelve items or fewer, and I didn't cop an attitude when the receptionist at the pool couldn't figure out how to ring up the sale for my family punch pass. But regardless of how tame our town seemed, I still wanted my kids to have some street smarts. I wanted to prepare them for potential dangers—obvious and hidden—that, as I was raised to believe, exist everywhere. I didn't want to scare them into thinking that they always need to be on guard; I just wanted them to understand that things are not always as they seem. At the very least, I thought they should know how to people watch.

When I was eight years old, my father and I watched a man in a brown leather club chair. We were in the lobby of the Statler Hotel, sitting in club chairs of our own. These weren't our usual seats, but we still had a good view of the reception desk. After he'd lit a first cigarette, my father nodded in the direction of the man across the room from us. We'd seen this man here before. He drummed his fingers on a copy of the *New York Post* folded on his lap, but never looked down at the headlines. He wore solid brown wing tips and a blue business suit. He had no tie clip or cuff links. I didn't notice a wedding ring or other jewelry. The man in the club chair was so inconspicuous that he stood out, but only if you happened to be spying on him. He could have been anyone—a bookie, a billionaire, an amnesiac, a thief—I couldn't begin to guess.

"What do you think he does for a living?" my father asked, gesturing with his cigarette in hand. "I'll give you a hint; he works for the hotel."

I could have gone through a roster of jobs—chef, bellman, concierge, janitor—but I couldn't explain why any of these people would be in business attire and stationed in the lobby. Then my father gave me another clue, "Check his ankles." The game was now in high gear. My father bowed his head as he flicked ash into the ashtray, and while I couldn't see his face, I knew he was concealing a smile.

The time I spent with my father in the lobby of the Statler Hotel was like so much other time we spent together. We watched people on subway platforms and park benches, in stores and in line at the deli. We watched them to learn a part of their story, the part that would intersect with our lives, if only for a split second, as we passed them on the street or maneuvered for a seat on the bus. We watched them to intuit their intentions and their intensity. But mostly we watched them because my father taught me and my brothers to always be on guard. The twenty or thirty minutes we sat in the Statler, we watched people for practice with nothing at stake. It was people watching in its purest form.

Trips to the Statler were on days when my father picked me up from elementary school. My school stood at a public transportation crossroads in midtown Manhattan. Within a few blocks in any direction you could find a local or express bus or subway to take you anywhere in the five boroughs. The route my father chose depended on three factors—weather, hunger, and time. On nasty days when he'd skipped lunch, we would fight the wind off the Hudson River to take the Seventh Avenue subway, our best chance to get back to the apartment in less than forty minutes. On nice days, when there was time to pick up a pretzel and a cream soda from a vendor along the park and still run errands, we would stroll the few blocks to catch any of the Eighth Avenue local subways. But on days when my father wasn't in any rush, we would take the M10 bus. The M10 stopped directly in front of the school, which made it convenient to catch, but it was the slowest transportation option home. On those days—when my dad would stop at the bottom of the granite steps of the school and not check his watch, not turn into the wind along the avenue—taking the M10 meant an afternoon with nothing but time on our hands. These were afternoons to be savored; these were the rare times when he had no pressing agenda. Stepping off the bus at the corner of Thirty-Fourth Street, we elbowed our way through a mix of commuters, shoppers, ticket scalpers, and street vendors. Somewhere along the block there was always a crooked game of three-card Monte. But when we stepped off the M10, we wouldn't stop at the card games to sort the cons from the marks, the lookouts from the bruisers; we'd walk up the few steps that led to the Statler Hotel's colonnade entrance and find a couple of seats in the lobby.

My father would pull out a pack of cigarettes and survey the lobby. He would point out a stranger—the woman by the newsstand, the man getting a shoeshine—and ask a simple question like "Does she like her job?" or "Did he work hard for a living or inherit all his money from his family?" The point wasn't to give a right answer, just a well-reasoned one. My father had taught me that the first, best clue was always the shoes—leather soles or rubber, overstretched or well fitted, dyed-to-match or off-the-shelf neutral? Next, I learned to scan for telltale belongings—luggage with locks, pocket rain ponchos, "I Love New York" T-shirts, walking sticks, diamond engagement rings, watch fobs, mismatched socks, and off-season linen. He also showed me how to observe people's behavior. Who deftly slipped folded bills as a tip? Who fumbled with their wallet? Who forgot the gratuity altogether? It was all information that told a story, and that story (true or not) told us something about the people we were watching. Whether I thought the woman by the newsstand was a dental hygienist in town for a convention or an Iowa farmer on the trail of a runaway child, I had to say why. And if I was sure the man getting his shoes shined was either an eccentric fur merchant or an out-of-work plumber, I had to have a good reason. In the next move in the game, my father would challenge my explanations. Did she really have the hands of a laborer? Did he behave like someone with money to burn? Any dreamer could tell a good story, but only someone with street smarts could back that story up with evidence.

The afternoon my father and I sat in the Statler lobby staring at the man in the leather club chair was an exception to our usual routine; he seemed to have insider information. I looked back at the stranger and tried to make the best of my latest clue—I studied his ankles. His feet were planted hip-width apart on the carpet. The cuffs of his pants draped slightly over the laces of his shoes. He didn't shift in his seat or cross his legs. His only movements were his drumming fingers and an occasional slow pan of the room. Nothing about his ankles (or any other part of him) brought me closer to knowing what his job was at the hotel. I had no reasonable guess, and said so.

"Do you see how one ankle looks a little thicker than the other?" my father asked.

I wasn't sure, but nodded yes. And then my father got up out of his chair and motioned that it was time to go home. We walked right by the man. This was my last chance to uncover something that would unveil his identity. He was clean-shaven. He had dark eyes and short-cropped hair. No jewelry. No disfiguring scars. He was as unassuming up close as at a distance. When we stepped out of the hotel and headed down the block, I demanded to know the answer. What did the man do for a living?

"He's the undercover security guard," my father said, matter-of-factly.

"But what about his ankles?" I said.

"That's where he's carrying his gun."

How could I have missed it? It was so obvious, once I knew. I thought about how he had glanced down at his newspaper, but never opened it. And how he had scanned the lobby, but without the expectant look of waiting for someone. I reeled from the knowledge that I had come in such close range of a man with a gun. It was staggering to think that danger could be so thinly cloaked. I took my father's hand and matched his step, not wanting to fall behind.

For me trips to the Statler were a game, but for my father it was serious business and had everything to do with who he was and where he'd come from. He had grown up black and poor in Harlem during the Depression. He lived in a tough neighborhood and ran with a tough crowd. His ability to size people up often meant the difference between getting beaten, killed, or off the hook. My brothers and I had an easier time; we lived in tame neighborhoods, attended private schools, and went on family vacations—things my father never had as a kid. For us the point of people watching was more academic than it had been for him growing up. But in his mind it was still primal. "Sugar," he often said to me, "it's important to always be on your toes because that's what gives you an edge." Even as a child I found his logic easy to follow—if you don't have the edge, then someone else does.

((

When I left New York City after college, I downsized my life by degrees—first moving to smaller and smaller cities and then to smaller and smaller towns. Each time I relocated, I got to know my neighborhood by ambling around, taking a new route to the store each day. In New York City, you are most vulnerable on the street, and the pleasure is rarely in "the going" but in "the getting there." In a small town, I could set out from my apartment without worrying so much about what was outside my door. I got to know my neighbors. I smiled at strangers. The farther I moved away from home and the longer I stayed away, the less convinced I was that my life was better or safer by being constantly on guard. When my father visited me in these towns, he seemed disappointed by the dwarfed skylines and the slow pulse of the streets. He'd shake his head and say, "People here are soft."

By the time my kids were born, my father was ill with Alzheimer's and his laser-like view of the world had blurred to a teary focus. He was too sick to tell my kids stories about what it was like when he'd grown up and why it was important to know the rules and tricks of people watching. Sharing those secrets had fallen to me. It was hard to know how much street smarts my kids needed in a place where the city bus runs past fields of pumpkins and piles of mint compost. My children sang and swung their arms when we walked downtown; they waved at people in the library because they thought they looked like people who lived on our street. When I was their age, I had been schooled in keeping a poker face, but I didn't want them to be that way, or at least, not exactly that way. I thought there was room for trust in their lives, as long as it included trusting their gut instincts. The anonymity of New York City had made it easy to sit and watch people; it was harder in a small town where taut aloofness and close scrutiny made you stand out rather then blend in. So, I adapted my father's people-watching techniques by asking my kids questions when we were out on errands to encourage them to take notice of their surroundings. I said things like, "Do you think the waitress smiles at all her customers?" or "What yummy meal could we cook with the groceries in that lady's shopping cart?" It felt like a less ambitious protocol than his, and I often wondered whether it was having any effect. But that day at the pool, I thought some dose of wariness had rubbed off when it seemed that my son had stopped to ask a question of his own: "Why is that man staring at my sister?" He didn't need to know the answer to realize that just the question had made him uneasy. And he didn't need to know why he felt uneasy to take action. When he wrapped his arms around Dahlia, I knew that he had noticed what I had, and that, I thought, was something to build on.

If my father had been at the pool, he likely would have thought I was pushing my luck, that I should have called the kids to my side, kept them there, and looked the man up and down as if I were memorizing his details. My father wouldn't have bought the argument that bad things don't happen in small towns; I might have tried it, but I wouldn't have made a convincing case because I didn't believe it myself. I could imagine the disappointed look he would have given me. It would have been the same one that he used to give me at the Statler Hotel when my explanations were hasty and unsound. I remembered how he would tilt his head back and exhale cigarette smoke before setting his eyes on me, waiting to see if I would recognize

⟨ Formula for Combustion

A series of lightning strikes to several electrical substations caused the 1977 New York City blackout, but my father blamed the heat. It was a sticky July night.

"It's all those goddamn air conditioners," he said as he looked out of our twelfth-story kitchen window into the inky darkness. I had been in the middle of watching an episode of *Baretta* when the TV image shrank to a dot. I stood next to my father and stared at our neighborhood, which had been transformed into a collection of blank boxes. Over the tops of the storefront brownstones on Eighth Avenue, the outline of the Empire State Building was a shadowy silhouette. If I had gazed up at the sky, I might have seen the Big Dipper or the Great Bear, but I wasn't used to looking for stars; the glare from the buildings always drowned them out.

I was eleven when the lights went out. For most New Yorkers, it had already been a tough year. The city was in a financial crisis and teetered on the verge of bankruptcy. With money going only to essential services, the streets got dirtier and the potholes got bigger. City-funded public health clinics closed, and HIV and tuberculosis cases started to rise. Teachers were laid off, and leaky roofs in schools got patched but not repaired. But I didn't notice those kinds of things as a kid. Mostly, I remember riding the subway with the windows, seats, and walls covered with graffiti and gang tags. And who can forget reading the headlines about the Son of Sam, who was on the loose in the city killing brunettes and mocking the police with rambling handwritten notes. That summer seven million people were looking over their shoulders and keeping an eye on anyone who looked suspicious in the streaky light creeping through the spray painted windows of the subway cars. For Yankees fans eager to escape their worries about murder and belt tightening, the 1977 season was strained with feuds and fallouts between players and management. That summer the city was on edge. And then the heat came.

In the weeks leading up to the blackout, the temperature hovered in the high eighties, which drove people to their stoops, terraces, and rooftops, looking for a breeze. During the day, the sun hung like a mirrored spotlight and supercharged the short tempers of people pushing past each other on the street. The heat radiated off the glass and steel surfaces of the buildings; you didn't want to touch anyone or anything. At night, the leftover air stayed warm and crept insidiously under doorways and between sheets, leaving anyone without an air conditioner awake and sweating into the small hours. Because there had been no rain, the streets turned thirsty and overcooked, and the city felt wrapped in a taut skin. On the day of the blackout, the temperature stretched into the nineties and during the stifling moments before the power failure, most New Yorkers wilted through the evening, waiting for a break from the sweating and the worrying. Hardship is a tinder that, under the right conditions, is quick to ignite, and that Wednesday night in July, New Yorkers were primed for something to happen.

At first we thought the problem was local; we thought, maybe we'd lost power because so many people had their goddamn air conditioners on in our neighborhood and that it had overtaxed our section of the grid. From our windows we could see long stretches to the north and south. Although it was dark everywhere we looked, it would be hours until we figured out that all five boroughs were without power.

I wasn't frightened when the lights went out; we had had outages before. But the combination of extremes—heat and darkness—unsettled me. I licked a divot of sweat from my upper lip.

"How long is it going to last?" I asked my mother.

No power also meant we had no water because the city's pumping stations were offline. Cool showers had been the only thing to make the nights bearable. "I'll never get to sleep," I said, turning the faucet handle to test the tap.

An hour into the blackout, my mother was still optimistic that the power would be on any minute, but as it neared midnight, she decided to salvage the contents of the freezer.

"We can't sleep anyway," she said, pulling out two already-melting cartons of ice cream. I reached for bowls, but she stopped me. "Just get spoons. We won't be able to do the dishes." That was my first clue that the blackout might last. For years afterward, I associated the darkness with the heat and remembered them starting and ending together. That just goes to show how time and circumstance can distort the truth—the blackout lasted twenty-five-hours, but the heat wave would drag on for ten days. Still, the association of the two set like a stain.

My brothers were driving home from a cross-country trip when the lights went out. They were in my father's maroon Chevy Impala with the windows rolled down. There was no air conditioning in the car, but at highway speed the warm air transformed into a cross breeze. As they approached the George Washington Bridge, the power failure cascaded across the boroughs. The Upper East and West Sides disappeared first and then the darkness spread south, engulfing Broadway, Midtown, and Chelsea, where we lived, before taking out Lower Manhattan. The last patches of light shining in the Bronx, Queens, Brooklyn, and Staten Island went dead a few moments later, leaving millions of people collectively blinking and reaching out their hands to rummage through drawers and cabinets for candles, flashlights, and batteries. In the moments leading up to the power-crippling lightning strikes, my brothers had divided their attention between the stream of taillights in front of them and the Manhattan skyline gleaming on the far shore of the Hudson River—up close and at a distance the view had been points of light. But when the skyline went black, taillights flashed red as drivers slowed or stopped their cars to get a better look at what they couldn't see. The city was gone.

"We thought we were at war," my brothers admitted later.

"Or worse," they said with a laugh. "That it was aliens."

But when they glanced behind them and saw that New Jersey was still aglow, they took it as a sign that the world wasn't ending; it just looked like it. Traffic backed up going over the bridge and once they crossed the river, cars inched and jostled across streets with no working traffic signals. They arrived at the apartment hours later and walked in to find my parents and me eating melting ice cream from the cartons. We gathered up our half-frozen rations and sat on the terrace to watch the scene on the street. We mostly saw taxis, which slowed and cautiously jockeyed for position at the intersections. Their headlights and roof-mounted medallion numbers were the only illuminations on the block; it made the taxis' yellow bodies stand out in the night like mechanical beasts on patrol.

Our Chelsea neighborhood was quiet that first night of the blackout, and my parents, brothers, and I went to bed wishing for electricity and rain. While we tried to find sleep in air so heavy you could hold it in your hand, people in other parts of the city were waking up to a riot that was breaking loose. In the Bronx, Brooklyn, and Queens, crowds formed, brandishing crowbars and kerosene cans. They woke their neighbors and advanced on stores with baseball bats and cement blocks. Neighborhoods erupted into chaos as thousands of people poured out of their stifling apartments to loot their local stores. Men and women of all ages pried open doors, shot out locks, and smashed plate-glass windows to get at whatever was within reach. Children stepped over debris to help their parents carry off goods or they stood back on the sidewalk to watch over younger siblings. People came with shopping carts and dollies to roll away TVs, furniture, and stereo equipment; they backed cars up to storefronts to load their trunks with clothes and small appliances. Inside the darkened stores, the atmosphere was like a bargain basement on Christmas Eve, with pushing and elbowing for this mirror or that record player. Fights broke out as people took apart businesses in a grabbing frenzy. Outside on street corners, looters set up ad hoc bazaars and resold their booty at discount prices for cash to all comers. The Commissioner of Police put the department's civil emergency plan into effect, and called all able-bodied officers to report to their precincts. But even if the city's twenty-five thousand active officers had put on their uniforms that night, they wouldn't have come close to managing the insurrection in the streets. Around the time we had gone to bed, the police already had made hundreds of arrests, and before the night was over the jails were filled to capacity. Once the stores were gutted of merchandise, the looters set buildings on fire in a roaring, anarchic display that engulfed whole blocks in smoke. The air became suffused with the pungent smell of burning plastic, fabric, paint, wood, and garbage. Some stores were spared the conflagration; others were ravaged. Nearly a thousand fires had been set, and by morning many were still burning, and people were still stealing.

"When folks get that hot, they explode," my father said after talking on the phone to friends and relatives in other parts of the city. The phone, the only appliance unaffected by the blackout, became a lifeline of information.

When I asked him why our neighborhood hadn't exploded, he didn't answer. Maybe he didn't know, or maybe he didn't know how to explain that sometimes when people feel so starved for options, they'll grab at whatever they can.

"Is that going to happen here?" I said.

"No," he said.

I didn't ask him how he could be so sure because I just wanted to believe him.

The formula for combustion is straightforward: a source, like a match or a spark, ignites an oxygenated fuel. In some circumstances, the trigger is not a single element but a complicated, hidden process. Although some explosions appear to spring up spontaneously and without cause, they are often the result of a long series of reactions. Long-time New York City residents shook their heads after the blackout, trying to understand that night's mayhem and comparing it to the orderly atmosphere of the previous power outage in 1965. That year, there had been only a handful of reports of looting, violence, and vandalism. When the lights flickered and died that time, it had been on a cool, autumn late afternoon. Storeowners, neighbors, and police and fire departments had had time in the daylight to secure homes and businesses, organize necessary supplies, and settle in for the thirteen hours without electricity. The city was financially sound then, and feelings of hopelessness were less entrenched. In 1977, the looting and arson happened in the poorest neighborhoods, where people faced Depression-era levels of unemployment and social safety nets had been clipped. The blackout took the city off guard in the middle of the night when, under the cover of darkness, any idea had seemed like a good idea. The morning after the melee, many blamed the chaos on the heat. But in the complex chemistry of the city's social, economic, and political life, the heat wasn't the cause—it was the accelerant.

After several hours in the dark, the Consolidated Edison power company managed to restore power to a few neighborhoods, but the majority of New Yorkers remained without electricity for a solid day. While over fifteen hundred store owners took stock of the ruins of their businesses and ladder companies around the city finished putting out the last smoldering fires from the previous night, my family's focus turned to more ordinary concerns, namely, flushing the toilets without running water. One of our local fire captains opened a hydrant on our block so that people could collect water, and I started a daylong chore of hauling sloshing buckets up twelve flights in pitch-black stairwells lit with candles. Each trip I emptied the bucket out to fill our bathtub. My shirt, shorts, and sneakers were soaked from sweat and the spray that rebounded from the hydrant. The stairwell steps and landings had puddles from buckets that had been tipped or dropped. It was slow, hot work, but I preferred it to staying in the apartment. My mother had drawn all the blinds closed to keep the sun out, but it insinuated itself between the metal slats. The light inside had a hoary, claustrophobic glow. My mother closed the windows to keep the hot air out, but with no electricity to run a fan, it was only a few degrees cooler inside than in the street. By midday, the temperature crept past ninety-two, and the air in the apartment tasted stale. My brothers went to the store to buy drinking water and whatever else they could find, while my mother threw out the most vulnerable contents of the refrigerator: egg salad, uncooked chicken breasts, mayonnaise, and everything from the freezer. She put a towel on the floor to soak up the steady drip from the refrigerator as it defrosted. My father spent the day at the community center he ran, standing guard to prevent any break-ins.

After a day of hauling water, I tossed and turned in bed with a sore back and tired arms. When I dragged myself into the kitchen the next morning, my mother was restocking the refrigerator. Soggy towels were still pushed up against it on the floor, but I could hear the appliance's motor and compressor humming. The blackout was over.

The lights came back on, but the heat didn't shut off. The fires burning in the boroughs were out, but the city felt beaten down and spent. The temperature climbed into the triple digits, so my mother and I went out to buy a watermelon; chilled slices were the best heat-penetrating treat. Walking home pushing the melon in a shopping wagon, we passed the neighborhood playground, where children—some shirtless, some in bathing suits, some stripped down to their underpants—darted back and forth under a sprinkler. The littlest ones collected water in sand pails and emptied them over their mother's flip-flops and sandals. The women, clustered together in the small shade of a tree, fanned themselves and sweated through the creases of their blouses and called out, "More, more," and the children giddily splashed their toes, ankles, and up to their knees, even. And the women didn't mind when their skirt hems and tops were dotted with water because when the thermostat climbs so high, heat incinerates the rules about what's allowed and what's not.

I didn't want to go back up to our apartment; I didn't want to wait for the watermelon to chill in the refrigerator. I edged toward the park's gate. "Just for a few minutes?" I said. But my mother pulled me away, and we continued on the path toward our building. Instead, that day and the days that followed, she let me thread the garden hose through the bathroom window and make my own sprinkler on the terrace. She usually never let me do this, but these weren't just any lazy summer days; the air still felt volatile, like anything might still happen. From the twelfth floor, I could see the playground. It was a shimmering island, the hottest place on the planet with its black asphalt and burning sands. The metal jungle gym and swings gleamed menacingly in the day's white sizzle. The sound of the children's laughter didn't reach me twelve stories up, which made their leaps through the sprinkler appear more frantic than playful. I passed the hose through the window so my mother could screw the end cap to the faucet. I heard the throaty squeak of the handle when she turned the cold water on. I listened for the hiss of pressure as the water snaked through the hose and watched it wriggle to life. It was hard for me—for anyone—to think further than each hot moment, but maybe if we could have glimpsed into the future it would have made the unfolding days of the heat wave easier to endure. We had no idea, for example, that the police would catch the Son of Sam by the end of the summer, that many of the looted businesses would slowly rebound, that the Yankees would win that year's World Series, or that the city would eventually claw its way back to fiscal solvency. All we had was the air, simmering like a madness and cooking us from the outside in. With no end in sight, I held the hose over my head, took a deep breath, and leaned into the shock that I knew was coming.

⟨⟨ A Lingering Sense of Place

On the Train in Oregon

"No more trains coming through these parts until tomorrow," the conductor says, warning passengers not to stray off if they decide to stretch their legs at the next stop. We are approaching Klamath Falls, the last smoking stop on the Coast Starlight before the train leaves Oregon and pushes south through the night into California. If you want to light up during the thirty-five-hour ride between Seattle and Los Angeles, you have to disembark at designated stations. I don't smoke, but I move toward the exit when the rail clacks slow and the brakes begin to hiss; I am eager for the night air. Heading down the narrow grate steps, I repeat the conductor's words: "These parts." They suggest the risk and romance I associate with the West. Or, I wonder, do we always idealize and brand the places we are not from?

Outside the air is crisp and the stars pinpoint an early spring sky. Sixty or so passengers spill out of the cars in straight lines and pool in the graveled area between the tracks and the darkened station building. At first, we are just a silent, random crowd stamping our feet against the cold. But as cigarettes emerge, neighbors turn to neighbors and lean into cupped hands, sheltering lit matches from the wind. As one person spreads the flame to another, strangers begin to shuffle into semi-circles, five or six smokers in each, drawn together by a shared craving.

I stand near an arc of young men who, between drags, compare how many beers they've had. To figure out who is the drunkest they calculate ratios of alcohol to distance to account for the fact that they boarded at different stations; they reach no conclusions. Despite their offhand manner, their accidental acquaintance has a precious character, as though they are something more than just a group of guys who met in the middle of the night on a train. Behind me, a woman reminisces about the good old days, when you could smoke wherever you wanted. Her voice rings with resentment and reverie; she speaks in the language of banishment. As I watch the groups hem closer I become aware of my outcast status; I am the nonsmoker, standing alone in the cold, staring. I re-board the train ahead of the others with a strange sense of longing, wanting to be part of that instant community, no matter how delicately impermanent. I console myself when I take my seat, knowing that while I am not of them, I am with them, sharing the misfit status of one who travels the rails by night.

Looking out the window, I see the shadowy outlines of the passengers, the burning butts of their cigarettes glowing like sparks from a campfire. I am drawn to the cinematographic familiarity of the scene, as if I am watching a movie of modern-day pioneers, circled up for protection and comfort. In 1890, the Census Bureau declared that the frontier region of the United States no longer existed. Rates of western migration could not be tabulated because there no longer was a clear axis dividing where we had been from where we were headed. Those who risked their lives to traverse the country did so for all kinds of reasons—land, trade, gold, religion—some running from their pasts, others running toward their futures, and everyone seeking to reinvent themselves. It's as though I glimpse that history now in the faces of the people from the train, dimly illuminated by the faint winking of distant stars. To look at us one might only see a group of people heading south to California, but the spirit of migration haunts these rails; it has followed us to this place, this moment, and calls out in a pitch barely audible to even the quietest mind.

When I told my mother I intended to move out West—where I knew no one and had no prospects—she looked at me as if I were a runaway, an escape artist, a dreamer. She reminded me that we take ourselves with us on any journey. But I already knew from experience that changing my zip code was no promise of a different fortune. I had lived in several cities, settling in some of them for a few years before moving on. She read my reluctance to put down roots as aimlessness and cautioned against moving to find myself. It was hard to explain to her that I wasn't looking for a place to know who I was, but who I might become.

At a Café in New Hampshire

Over tea and sweets, I say, "I once kicked a woman in the stomach for a taxi." I intend the remark to put my most recent misdemeanor into perspective, but it only seems to alarm my two girlfriends. We've just come from the movies, where I hotly scolded a woman for talking. For the first hour of the film I had maintained suburban politeness, ignoring the woman's running commentary. It's hard to say what finally broke my reserve, what finally triggered me to whip around and growl, "Jesus, can you just give it a rest already?" Even in the dim, flickering light I could tell she was startled, I think less by my words and more by the fact that I was standing halfway out of my seat. She called me one of those people who should mind their own business. I thought I saw her look me up and down, judge me; I thought I heard in her voice that same tight tone I knew from childhood, when someone mumbled "spic" behind my back. I countered with, "Who the hell do you think you are?" I don't remember what I shouted next but I know I was leaning over the back of my seat and pointing. My friends never turned their heads; they kept their eyes fixed on the screen and pretended nothing was out of the ordinary. Now, after hearing about the taxi, they eye me apprehensively, as if they misjudged the level of threat in the movie theater. I lightly offer the only explanation I have: "That's what you get from a New Yorker."

Mulling over this flip explanation for my behavior, I consider the tendencies of place—the expectations, values, and behaviors of where we live that evolve over time and, with each generation, penetrate the soil that we walk, work, and crave. When we sink roots in a place, we take up these tendencies, like plants tapping nutrients and, for better or worse, grow accustomed to what our environment offers and demands. Growing up in Manhattan, I went to the movies with reverence, eager for entry into a fantasy world where apartments were cockroach-free and janitors passed up opportunities to expose themselves to little girls waiting for elevators. I suspect that my fellow moviegoers, slotted like congregants into rows of theater seating, were seeking similar deliverance. I think that's why the crowd was always so quick to verbally punish anyone whispering, chatting, coughing, or even just chewing loudly. Silence was venerated; it was the vessel of escapism. And while I can't remember anyone standing up and waving an angry fist to restore quiet, it doesn't mean it never happened.

Sipping my tea, I wonder about the difference between the historical humus of New Hampshire and New York City, the two media in which my friends and I were raised. The Dutch founded Manhattan as New Amsterdam, a market-driven colony where all personal practices were tolerated, provided they didn't interfere with profitability, and where magistrates sought to manage, but not outlaw, music, drinking, and gambling. New England, by contrast, guided by colonial Puritan codes of morality, looked upon leisure with misgivings. The first New Hampsherites, no doubt, wrestled with the notion of entertainment in terms of its threat to piety and propriety. Now, one of my friends raises a foot alongside the table and asks, "So, how do you kick someone in the stomach, anyway?" I recount the story of the taxi, emphasizing farce over force, and then quickly change the subject to avoid what seems like the next logical question: What drives a person to have such instincts? I believe we are in part the products of our environment. But how do you measure the effect of place on the body? In microns, in miles, in millennia?

On the Subway in New York City

On the subway platform, waiting for the number 1 train, I tug on my son Meilo's hood, pulling him a few yards to the right. He resists, saying, "I'm not a baby." A few years ago, when we were last in New York City, he stormed off in a tantrum in the middle of the Times Square station—a small boy from a small town in Oregon, caught in the hungry press of commuters. I kept a tight eye on him, but let some distance open up between us, just enough to make him feel the first panicked twinges of separation so I could later make him understand—in a manner most visceral—how dangerous that kind of behavior is. Two police officers noticed him wandering, and then saw me. They gestured with their hands, as if to say, "Is he with you?" I nodded and waved the officers back. The whole time Meilo was unaware that he was being watched—by me, by the police, and very possibly by others who didn't have his best interests in mind. His yellow anorak stood out against the cold shades of grey concrete and rusting girders; it was a beacon of his innocence. He's three years older now; he's learned his lesson and thinks he doesn't need his mother to push and pull him around. I tell him that I pushed and pulled him not because of his age but because the man standing behind us was taking off his pants. Meilo doesn't believe it until he glances cautiously over his shoulder. "How did you know?" he asks, hemming a little closer to me.

I've struggled over the years to explain to him the practical meaning of street smarts when we are at home in our small college town, where there is little demand for constant vigilance. Our trips to New York City are a chance to practice the basics—anticipating the actions of others, seeing behind you without turning around, looking past people without looking directly at them. When he asks me how I learned these tricks, I tell them my parents taught me, but really it's much more than that; it's an unseen saturation of cues—how to act and react—that sinks in through the pores and pulses just below the surface of the skin. It requires more than an occasional visit to understand that the city doesn't just grow on you, it grows into you. But Meilo is not from these parts; he is only passing through. When I look at him I see the distance between being of a place and from it.

When the subway pulls into the station, Meilo asks if we can ride in the front car. We stand by the window next to the conductor's booth and watch as the subway enters the tunnel and leaves the station. The light ahead dims, but never goes black; bare bulbs in wire fixtures hanging from concrete pillars peel past and mark our speed. After only a few minutes, the mouth of the tunnel widens, illuminating the platform at the next station. The screech of the brakes is metal on metal. We watch the stations come in and out of focus, our destination always just within sight. I feel comforted by this predictability. On the Coast Starlight I spent hours looking out of the darkened windows, passing through the trailing edge of the Cascade Mountains where it was impossible to tell where Oregon ends and California begins. As the cars snaked through the night, I would catch glimpses of lights and each time was convinced we were nearing a town. But really I was seeing the locomotive's headlight projected forward on the tracks as it edged around a sharp bend. I felt uneasy only knowing where I was headed and not where I was. But here on the subway I am at home, even though this city is the place I chose to leave or maybe precisely because I take it with me wherever I am.